Penguin Handbooks

The Complete Barbecue Book

James Marks was born in London and received his education in Scotland and England. His career in selling and marketing has involved him in many diverse products such as lawn sprinklers, window blinds, waste disposal units and reinforced concrete structural framework, but for many years he has concentrated his complete attention on the world of barbecues. He is presently Marketing Director of a major barbecue manufacturing company.

During the past decade he has participated in numerous live radio and television broadcasts on the subject and he is continually giving lectures and demonstrations to a wide variety of audiences both here and abroad.

His best-selling *Barbecues*, first published by Penguin in 1977, was brought out in a revised and updated edition in 1984.

James Marks lives with his wife and youngest son in a delightful half-converted stable in a small hamlet situated in beautiful countryside near the Northamptonshire/Leicestershire border.

D0488311

The Complete Barbecue Book

Jim Marks

Penguin Books

Penguin Books Ltd, Harmondsworth, Middlesex, England
Viking Penguin Inc., 40 West 23rd Street, New York, New York 10010, U.S.A.
Penguin Books Australia Ltd, Ringwood, Victoria, Australia
Penguin Books Canada Ltd, 2801 John Street, Markham, Ontario, Canada L3R 1B4
Penguin Books (N.Z.) Ltd, 182–190 Wairau Road, Auckland 10, New Zealand

First published 1985
Copyright © James Marks, 1985
All rights reserved
Printed in Great Britain by
Butler & Tanner Ltd, Frome, Somerset
Typeset in Linotron Trump Mediaeval by
Rowland Phototypesetting Ltd, Bury St Edmunds, Suffolk

Contents

List of Colour Plates

List of Text Figures

Acknowledgements

Heading the honours list must be my wife Brenda, for not only did she manage to decipher, and then type, the scribbled manuscript of this book but, together with her mother, prepared all the food for cooking on the barbecue. It is perhaps worthy of mention that all the food photographed for this book was cooked on a barbecue of one type or another and not one item ever saw the inside of an oven! Neither was any 'cosmetic' (such as glycerine) applied to make the meats look more appetizing. My second vote of thanks must go to Geoff Stanton, who did such a marvellous job in photographing all the various dishes and I am only sorry that many of the superb photographs taken could not be included in the book. Next in line for a pat on the back is David Butler, for executing a series of strong and informative line drawings. Mr Bowers of Stuart Bates Butchers, Market Harborough, supplied me with British meat of superlative quality and his crown roast was a work of art before it became the mouth-watering roast depicted in Plate 4. While on the subject of meat I would like to thank the Meat Promotion Executive of the Meat and Livestock Commission for their generous assistance.

I am very grateful for the trouble taken by Real Flame at the Gas Log Fire Emporium, George Street, London, for getting together a selection of barbecues and accessories from their stock for us to photograph. Finally I would like to thank the following for their kind help in providing information: the New Zealand High Commission, the Australian High Commission, the South African Embassy, the United States Embassy, the British Chicken Information Service, the British Turkey Federation, McCormick Spices, the New Zealand Information Bureau and Alcan Bacofoil.

Introduction

The British are by nature rather conservative when it comes to disporting themselves in public. We were, and perhaps still are, rather loath to follow the continental habit of taking refreshment, weather permitting, outside rather than inside the café, restaurant or pub. It was perhaps inevitable, however, that we would eventually join the ranks of those who had succumbed to the tempting aroma of food sizzling over a bed of hot charcoal. In fact, barbecuing as a pastime made several false starts in Britain before the bug finally bit. During the late fifties and early mid sixties a few retailers, mostly London-based departmental stores, imported modest quantities of barbecues from North America. Usually of a rather flimsy and basic design, they were offered with a certain amount of trepidation because sales during those early days depended almost entirely on the whims of the weather. If, as sometimes happened, the sun appeared only intermittently, the retailer would find himself with most of his stock still on his hands at the end of the season. Having burnt his fingers once, or perhaps twice, the store buyer was naturally reluctant to repeat the exercise. In any event, apart from the trendy middle-class 'back-to-nature' brigade, customers for the latest new-fangled import from America tended to be relatively thin on the ground. As a consequence, the barbecue, having proved itself to be somewhat of a commercial flop, was more or less written off as a serious contender for a share of the growing UK market for leisure goods.

After remaining in the doldrums for several years, barbecues began to reappear on the British scene during the late sixties and early seventies. Their reappearance coincided with a gradual change of attitude towards eating outdoors. This change was almost certainly linked to the phenomenal increase in the number of people now able, thanks to the package-tour operators, to take their annual holiday abroad. Holidaymakers found they enjoyed eating their snacks and meals on the pavement or terrace and many who went to Spain also took the opportunity of attending one of the large-scale, highly organized barbecues which today are a regular attraction of the Spanish holiday scene.

The steadily growing popularity of barbecuing was given a decided boost by the glorious long hot summer of 1976 followed by the Jubilee celebrations the next year, but in my opinion the point at which one could say that barbecuing had firmly established itself in Britain was that wonderful July day in 1981 when we celebrated the wedding of Prince Charles and Princess Diana. It seemed to me at the time that every town and village – and many individual streets – included a barbecue in its celebration programme. The one that I helped to organize went on into the small hours, having started early in the afternoon. Splendid lively music, good company and the nose-twitching, mouth-watering aroma wafting out on to the balmy evening air made it an unforgettable experience.

According to trade estimates, sales of barbecues, charcoal and barbecue accessories in the United Kingdom during the past decade have increased twentyfold. Despite this, we are still a very long way behind West Germany where, with a similar population, around 1·5 million barbecues are sold per annum. However, at the present rate of increase in sales, Britain should have caught up by the late eighties.

Who knows, when, where and by whom the first piece of meat was cooked over hot coals. Like most great discoveries, the dawn of barbecuing probably resulted from a happy combination of accident and chance. The archaeologist and historian can each point to plentiful evidence that man has been perfecting his open fire cooking techniques for centuries past. During a recent visit to Bayeux I went to see the famous Tapestry, which shows the farewell party

Photo: Giraudon (with permission of the town of Bayeux)

given by Odo, Bishop of Bayeux, for his liege lord William Duke of Normandy just before William and his army set off across the Channel in 1066. I was fascinated to see that busy servants are offering the guests a selection of spit-roasted chicken, kebabs and sausages all cooked, it would appear, on the Norman equivalent of an open barbecue.

The appeal of barbecuing can be illustrated by the remarks made by Peter Kronberg, head chef at a large London hotel, when he was interviewed by the *Daily Mail* in 1982, just after he had been voted 'best chef in the land'. Mr Kronberg said, 'My neighbours think I am absolutely mad because the way I relax is by having a barbecue. It doesn't matter what time of the year it is. Last January in the snow I was out there barbecuing some new-season salmon escalopes. It was something very simple – just a little tomato vinaigrette on the side . . .'

In fact all of us, when at the helm of a barbecue, can become 'master chefs' in the eyes of our family and friends. Every speculative prod of the meat as it is being barbecued to perfection, every brush stroke as we apply our own 'special-recipe' sauce to the spare-ribs, every earnest gaze seeking to gauge the state of the charcoal fire, will serve to engage the rapt attention of the hungry, and therefore extra-appreciative, audience.

One of the reasons behind the phenomenal growth in the popularity of barbecuing during recent years is that more and more people realize that

holding a barbecue party is an ideal way to entertain family and friends inexpensively. It is not difficult, using the right equipment, to conjure up a superb three-course barbecued meal using the choicest cuts of meat, fresh vegetables, etc., and a couple of glasses of tolerable wine per head, at about a third of the price charged for a similar meal in a good restaurant. Or the guests can bring along their own steaks, etc., while the host provides the liquid refreshment and, of course, the cooking equipment.

The fact that one can feed a large number of people very well indeed at a fairly modest cost makes barbecues popular with clubs, charitable organizations, and so on. An evening of good food and good company usually means that event organizers can rely on the same people supporting the function the following year. A few hints and wrinkles on organizing large barbecue parties are given on pp. 62–7.

The barbecue chef can alter the venue to wherever he, she or the guests desire – garden patio, beach, river bank, or one of the growing number of countryside picnic areas now being opened up by enlightened councils. Most, if not all, of these specially designated areas, with their fixed tables and benches, are ideal for lunchtime barbecues. Some sites have permanent barbecues for the use of visitors and therefore only require the itinerant chef to take along charcoal, firelighter, food and drink.

The party's location will obviously have a strong influence on its success or otherwise. Claudia Roden wrote feelingly in her marvellous book *Picnic* of memorable meals in the Seychelles Islands, with sea breezes and clear waters providing a perfect setting for the luscious smell of pork roasting on a fruit-wood fire. As far as I am concerned, and I believe this goes for most people, the best time of day to mount a barbecue party is the evening – preferably a Saturday evening because having forewarned the neighbours (better in fact to have them there joining in the noise) – the party can then run on into the early hours of the following morning. Even if not actually being used for cooking, the barbecue at night makes a great focal point, reminiscent perhaps of scout and guide camp-fires. It's worth bearing in mind, when planning your late evening/early morning barbecue that appetites in the open air have great powers of revival, so the guests who swore they could not eat another thing at 9 p.m. will without doubt be mildly ravenous at around midnight (or before). Bearing this in mind you will be well advised to keep the barbecue in a state of readiness at all times, i.e. like the Olympic flame, do not let it go out until the games are over! Also make sure you have a back-up supply of burgers and sausages in the refrigerator.

For most people the word barbecue conjures up visions of fat, sizzling sausages, succulent steaks or juicy spare-ribs, but for many barbecuing must be an anathema – I refer of course to vegetarians. However, there are now several commercial dry non-meat mixtures available which can be quickly made up into tasty burgers or cutlets. My family and I are not vegetarians but we enjoy eating the occasional 'vege-burger'. There are recipes in the fruit and vegetable recipe section for the vegetarian chef.

Diet, calorie, nutrition, slimming, cholesterol – losing weight while retaining an interest in the food one is eating is perhaps the name of the game. Meat grilled over hot charcoal has a lot going for it for calorie counters. For example, the fat falling away from a pork chop will reduce the chop's calories by well over 40 per cent. The same pork chop when fried will only lose something in the order of 30 per cent of its calories. A fully barbecued meal comprising a 6 oz (170 g) pork chop, 3 oz (85 g) portions of Brussels sprouts and carrots plus a 7 oz (200 g) baked potato adds up to approximately 440 calories. For a sweet there are several low-calorie choices but the slimmer could try barbecued spiced banana, which, with the addition of its level teaspoon of honey, would add less than 80 calories. The whole meal would amount to little more than 50 per cent of a 1,000-calories-a-day slimming diet. Barbecued food can therefore help the slim to stay slim and the 'fatty' to enjoy losing weight.

With today's modern barbecue equipment it is not difficult to produce the variety of gourmet dishes one would normally associate with the kitchen oven or microwave. And all that fresh air, laden with the aroma of sizzling food, works wonders on the appetite.

1 The Barbecue

Selecting the Right Equipment

Before setting out to purchase your first barbecue, assuming at this point you are intending to buy a portable unit rather than build a permanent one, I suggest you sit down and make a list of all the factors that will influence your choice. By so doing you should arrive at the garden centre or store with a fairly accurate idea of what your requirements are. Otherwise you could end up buying something unsuitable that will rot away unused at the bottom of the garden and, worse still, you and your family could become disenchanted with barbecuing.

So what are the basic decisions to be made before purchasing a barbecue? In fact, when you consider them they are not greatly different from those you would make before purchasing a gas or electric cooker, i.e. its capacity, its design, its cooking abilities and the price you are prepared to pay. One important difference is that there are stringent rules governing the design of a cooker – be it gas or electric. Minimum safety requirements have to be observed before it can be offered for sale. Unfortunately, barbecues are a different kettle of fish in that apart from the one or two electric barbecues on offer, and to a lesser extent the gas barbecues, no rigid codes are applied; I regret to say that there is still an awful lot of rubbish about masquerading as barbecues. Some offer little merit other than their low prices and are no more, in many cases, than cake tins on legs. Should you decide to purchase one of these very basic low-cost units do check that they are sufficiently stable to support the bed of hot charcoal and a food-laden grill safely. Too many barbecues, and the cheapies are not the only guilty ones in this respect, tend to sway dangerously when the fire-bowl is given even the slightest nudge. Also, it is obviously more difficult to cook successfully on a barbecue with a shallow fire-bowl (with no air vent) and very limited adjustment of the food grill above the fire-bed.

Having made up your mind how much you can afford to pay for your barbecue, you must decide how many people you will *normally* be catering for. In my opinion it is hardly worthwhile taking into account that odd

1. Universal (three bowl), p. 11
2. Universal (two bowl), p. 11
3. Universal (single bowl), p. 11
4. Wagon (hooded model), p. 10
5. DIY kit, p. 17

6. Electric, p. 25
7. Brazier, p. 7
8. Wagon (open grill), p. 10
9. Hibachi (double grill), p. 3

10. Gas, p. 23
11. Rectangular covered, p. 10
12. Boat, p. 5
13. Kettle, p. 8

Accessories featured in the photograph include rib rack, fish broilers, steak broiler, shish-kebab frame, tongs, bellows, garden lights, barbecue burning woods and herbs, a jumbo-sized rotisserie (to fit the open-grill wagon unit) and a roast holder.

occasion when you decide to invite a crowd along for a beano, for you can usually borrow an extra barbecue on those occasions. For those who can't make up their minds about size the solution could be the new Universal barbecue. Its unique modular system allows the owner to build on and expand the barbecue's capacity (see p. 11).

There is a very wide selection of models for open grilling. Some of these allow a rotisserie to be fitted and some include a rotisserie as a standard accessory. Then there are a number, some circular, some square shaped, that feature a cover (lid) in their design, thus enabling the chef to roast large joints as well. Should you fancy one of the increasingly popular gas-fired models (see p. 23), you can choose between those with single burners and those with double burners. The food is cooked, as above, by grilling, spit-roasting and oven roasting. If you prefer cooking by electricity, you can buy one of the electric barbecues.

The best way of finding out about the cooking performance of a particular type of barbecue is to attend a demonstration or ask friends who have one already.

Charcoal-burning Barbecues

Fully Portable

Many first-time barbecuers for economic or 'cash and caution' reasons ('until I know I am going to enjoy barbecuing and the taste of barbecued food I am not going to splash out on an elaborate job') will start by purchasing a small barbecue. Others who already own a large open brazier or covered barbecue may want to buy a compact fairly lightweight unit for picnics and beach parties.

Some of the barbecues described below are simply scaled-down versions of the standard 'semi-portable' models and therefore incorporate similar design features – adjustable grills, windshields and rotisseries. (Unless one is contemplating spit-roasting something the size of an immature pigeon it must be said that most rotisseries on fully portable barbecues are no more than rather ineffectual status symbols.)

Hibachis

For many people the word hibachi epitomizes the art of barbecuing. Not surprising, perhaps, bearing in mind that millions are sold throughout the world each year. Hibachi is not a trade-name; it is of Japanese origin and means fire-box, fire-bowl or, simply, brazier. Unfortunately, the intense competition amongst Far Eastern producers to capture a share of the market has resulted in some manufacturers churning out large quantities of gim-crack. Good-quality hibachis can be bought at remarkably low prices from garden centres and stores – but beware of bargains such as a double grill unit at the price you would normally expect to pay for three or four 8 oz steaks!

Hibachis are now available in a variety of shapes and sizes. Rarely seen in Britain, but very popular in the United States, are mini-hibachis 4–5 inches (10–12 cm) in diameter, used primarily to grill small skewered appetizers. The largest circular hibachis, free-standing and usually wheeled, are around 16 inches (41 cm) in diameter; the largest square ones are about 16 inches square (41 cm²). However, the most popular shape is still the rectangular version, which has changed very little in the past forty years or so, other than the development of two- and three-grill versions; the single-grill hibachi has lost ground to the double- and triple-grill units, probably because it is too limited to cope with a party of more than two or three people. The double-grill unit measures approximately 10 × 17 inches (25 × 43 cm) and the triple-grill unit approximately 10 × 27 inches (25 × 69 cm).

Hibachis have traditionally been manufactured from cast iron, but during the past few years all-steel versions have appeared on the scene. Unlike the cast-iron hibachi, the cooking grills on these new barbecues are made from plated wire. Some designs incorporate a separate ashbox and a hinged fire-bowl to make cleaning and ash disposal easier.

Grills on both the ancient and modern versions are adjustable to three different levels. The grill on the circular cast-iron hibachi is adjusted simply by rotating it up or down. All hibachis have draught-control vents situated in the side of the fire-bowl to assist the ignition of the charcoal and thereafter to help control the rate of burning.

Check Points

- Deeper fire-bowls generally mean better quality and better cooking control. Look for hibachis with a fire-bowl at least 3 inches (7·5 cm) deep.
- Having purchased one of the traditional cast-iron hibachis it is a sound idea to check the contents of the carton before leaving the store. Cast iron, especially the delicate grills and charcoal grates, can easily be damaged in transit.

The Brasero

Very similar in size to the single-grill hibachi is the Mexican brasero. Although very popular in the United States, the brasero, which takes the form of a hollow sculpted head that has, as it were, been trepanned to allow a small food grill to sit on top, the mouth wide open to give good draught for the charcoal fire, has not caught on here. The fact that the brasero is made in either terracotta or hard-fired pottery probably has something to do with it, because, apart from the problems of transport, pottery when subjected to high temperatures will often crack and break.

Picnic Barbecues

As the name suggests, picnic barbecues are suitable for taking with you to a picnic. However, what might qualify as a picnic barbecue for the car owner may be highly impracticable for the cyclist whose boot, as it were, rests upon his back.

The picnic unit comes in a wide variety of shapes and sizes. If they have a round open brazier shape their diameter should be in the 14–16 inch (36–41 cm) range if they are going to be easily portable, although an 18 inch (45 cm) diameter brazier barbecue can be transported if it is equipped with fairly short, folding, screw-in or telescopic legs.

A new type of picnic barbecue has a 16 inch (41 cm) diameter fire-bowl connected to a circular base by a telescopic tube, so that the fire-bowl can be locked into position at various heights to suit both the short and tall. The maximum working height is 36 inches (91 cm). Although many picnic barbecues are round, we are seeing more of the continental-designed fold-down barbecues which look like – and take up about the same amount of space as – a small brief-case. When unfolded for action their legs swing down to give a fairly stable platform.

One occasionally comes across very small, very basic and very cheap picnic barbecues comprising a shallow rectangular or circular tray, made of thin sheet metal, to hold the charcoal and a hinged wire-frame support, which also incorporates the food grill. These are almost in the same category as the disposable barbecues, rarely seen nowadays, which are specifically designed to be used once and then thrown away.

Barbecues on Boats

There are a few barbecues on the market that have been specifically designed for use on board any sailing or powered craft that has a sturdy railing round the deck. These barbecues are clamped, via a support bracket, to the railing stanchion, thus allowing them to be hung outboard of the vessel.

I well remember using one a few years ago on board a large pleasure steamer cruising up and down the Thames. Despite the choppiness of the water and the boat's movement, all the kebabs and chops remained safely on the grill.

The reason for this small miracle was the barbecue's suspension between gimbals, allowing the cooking surface to remain constantly in the horizontal position. A further bonus with this particular barbecue is that it can be simply lifted off its support bracket and taken on shore for a picnic.

Table-top Barbecues

Fully portable barbecues with short legs are sold as 'table-top' barbecues. One should try to avoid, whenever possible, using a barbecue with very short legs at ground level. It is uncomfortable, and therefore not conducive to safety, bearing in mind it contains hot coals and hot food. The best place for it is on a table which is stable and strong enough to take the weight, preferably large enough to accommodate the barbecue plus a variety of condiments, tools, plates, and so on, and with a heat-resistant surface. Failing the latter, one should place the barbecue on top of a piece of heat-resistant sheeting.

Check Points

- Whenever possible buy a picnic barbecue that incorporates an air vent in its fire-bowl. Without an air vent it is more difficult to light the charcoal fire and, on a still day, it can be a chore keeping the fire going.
- If the barbecue you are buying has legs that are clipped or screwed into position, satisfy yourself as far as possible that they will be stable when the barbecue is fully loaded with charcoal and food. Give it the 'wobble' test – gently nudge the fire-bowl to see how far it oscillates.
- Ensure that the model you intend to buy allows you to add charcoal to the fire without disturbing or upsetting the food on the grill.
- If the barbecue has a wind-up mechanism for raising and lowering the food grill, try to check that it will do so when fully laden with food.
- Check that the bars of the food grill are close enough together to prevent small sausages falling through.

Semi-portable

The term 'semi-portable' is meant to cover those barbecues which lie between the fully portable, lightweight models discussed above and the permanent built-in structures. Most will stay permanently on the garden patio or in the beer-garden of the local pub. Generally speaking, they are family-size but some, aided perhaps by a useful accessory, are designed to cope with food for twenty or more people. Each of the barbecue types featured below is available in several permutations – the choice is wide.

Brazier Barbecues

The name brazier speaks for itself, although in most instances the circular fire-bowl of this type of barbecue – unlike the street brazier of the night watchman – is unperforated. Brazier barbecues, also known as open-top barbecues, are one step up from the smaller picnic versions in that the circular grills range from 18 to 26 inches (46 to 66 cm) in diameter.

Nearly all brazier fire-bowls are made from sheet metal. Generally speaking, the bowl is supported by three tubular legs that screw in, bolt on or clip in. Nowadays most models are wheeled for easier handling. Brazier barbecues usually incorporate a windshield (sometimes of stainless steel) designed to accommodate a rotisserie and/or a slot-in food grill. With this type of barbecue, especially the larger units, my personal preference is for one which has a food grill that rotates on its axis. This allows the food to be quickly and easily spun away from a specially prepared 'hot spot' on the fire-bed – particularly useful if the fats dropping from the meat are starting to create a flare-up. The up-and-down adjustment of the rotating food grill on some models is carried out by turning a handle, on others by spinning the grill on its threaded spindle. Some of the better-quality, more expensive models have removable cast-iron grates on which the charcoal fire is supported. Most brazier barbecues come complete with a spit, but it is usually necessary to purchase a separate battery-driven motor to operate this.

Hooded Barbecues

Shallow windshields are no match for a capricious wind. The advent of the hooded barbecue, in essence a brazier with something akin to a pram hood clamped on the edge of the fire-bowl, has helped to solve the problem.

The hood has two functions: first, to protect the food cooking on the grill from the cooling breezes and at the same time to help prevent smoke getting in the faces of the chef and guests; and, second, to provide a stable support for a rotisserie unit.

A few years ago it was relatively easy to find hooded barbecues that incorporated a warming compartment inside the upper area of the hood – a useful place to keep plates and cooked food warm. Warming ovens now seem to be the preserve of a few wagon barbecues, but one can still of course place plates on top of the hood to take up some of the warmth from the charcoal burning in the fire-bowl below.

Virtually all hooded barbecues are of sheet metal with a diameter ranging from 22 to 24 inches (56 to 61 cm).

The Barbecue

'Two-way' Barbecues

Popular with continental barbecue chefs, and gaining in popularity here, is a barbecue that, like a TV set, has a vertical and horizontal hold. The 'two-way' type of barbecue is designed to be used either in the normal horizontal position for grilling steaks, chops, burgers, etc., or with the fire-bowl in the vertical position for spit-roasting; with the fire situated behind the spit-roast, fats will drop on to the drip tray, usually made of stainless steel, positioned directly beneath the meat. The problems arising from flare-up are therefore virtually eliminated, although occasionally a sudden build-up of heat may cause excessive fat to spurt back on to the hot bed of charcoal.

There are several variations on the 'two-way' theme to choose from. Some models give a wide choice of positions in which to locate the spit, thus allowing one to cook joints of different sizes or to place the food further away from the fire-bed to cook less quickly.

Although continental in origin, many of the 'two-way' barbecues are shipped in from the Far East. These units tend to be manufactured from cast iron, although pressed steel or steel plate versions are available.

Most of the new designs can be folded down for easy transportation and storage.

Check Points

- If buying a brazier or hooded barbecue check
  (a) the fire-bowl has no sharp edges, i.e. that the edge is 'rolled' over;
  (b) it passes the 'wobble' test (p. 6);
  (c) the grill wind-up mechanism, if it has one, works smoothly and positively;
  (d) the wind-shield or hood covers at least 50 per cent of the fire-bowl.

- Check the food grill to make sure it is well chromed and has a substantial feel to it. (Some grills are more reminiscent of the bars of a budgie cage.) The bars of the grill should be close enough together to prevent small sausages from falling through.

- The quality of spits varies considerably. Check that the spit feels sturdy enough to support a couple of medium-weight chickens without bending unduly. Try tightening the fixing bolts on both spit forks. The thread on these tends to strip easily on the cheap rotisseries, making them useless.

- Before buying a 'two-way' barbecue check that the mechanism for adjusting the unit from the vertical to the horizontal position – and vice versa – works smoothly and that the desired position is firmly held.

Kettle Barbecues

No one has yet been able to give me a satisfactory explanation as to how the circular kettle barbecue got its name. This type of barbecue first saw light of day in the mid-West of America just over thirty years ago. In the intervening years it has become one of the biggest selling and most popular barbecues in North America and during the past five years or so it has become increasingly well known in the European market.

There are several competitive makes of the kettle barbecue available and they all share one distinctive feature, the semicircular lid which sits on the lower bowl. On some models the lid is hinged and on others it is completely separate from the lower bowl. The lid always has an adjustable vent and a handle, usually made of hardwood. The bowl itself varies greatly. One model has an ashpan fitted inside the bottom of the bowl; others have the ashpan fitted outside. The 'insiders' say that their method avoids the problem of wind spreading the fine ash about and the 'outsiders' say that their method makes ash disposal easier and also allows the air to circulate more freely.

Another difference lies in the methods used to control the air passing into the lower fire-bowl. Most models use three separately controlled air vents (similar to the one used in the lid), but a recent ingenious variation involves the use of a single lever that not only opens and closes all three vents simultaneously but also sweeps accumulated ashes into the ashpan.

All kettle barbecues, with the exception of a 14½ inch (37 cm) diameter picnic model, have three tubular legs and are wheeled for mobility. The most popular sizes are 18½–22½ inches (47–51 cm) in diameter but larger models exist – up to a truly massive 37 inches (94 cm).

Most kettle units are made from steel, usually covered inside and out with porcelain enamel, but a range made from spun aluminium was recently launched. Both body finishes are weather-proof although the chrome-plated metalwork that is part of every model does suffer from being exposed to the weather. Another common feature of kettle barbecues is that they all incorporate a grill to support the charcoal. The grill, or grate, is situated in the lower region of the fire-bowl – well protected from breezes.

Perhaps the major reason for the kettle's popularity is that, once its lid is in position, it will perform exceptionally well in all weathers. Another advantage, not shared by most other types of barbecue, is that one can exert a fairly high degree of control over the food while it is being cooked. This is done by closing or opening the air vents, to adjust the heat level. With the lid in position the heat is reflected from all the inside surfaces of the barbecue, so that the food is cooked evenly.

A gas-fuelled version is available.

Check Points

- Ensure that the lid is reasonably close fitting and is not distorted.
- Open and close all the air vents to ensure they are easy to move.

Square Covered Barbecues

Also very popular in the United States, and becoming increasingly so in Great Britain, is the square covered barbecue (sometimes referred to as a square kettle) which works on the same principle as a round kettle – the hinged cover turns the barbecue into an outdoor oven and adjustable air vents allow one to control the temperature of the charcoal fire. When in the fully open position the hinged cover acts as a windshield and in this mode the barbecue's design allows a rotisserie to be installed.

The food grill on some models can be adjusted to various heights by control levers. The same levers can also be used to tilt the grill, thus allowing steaks to be cooked to different degrees of readiness (doneness) simultaneously.

Sizes of the square covered barbecues vary from around 19 inches (48 cm) to 25 inches (64 cm).

All models are wheeled. A gas-operated version is available.

Check Points

- Ensure that the hinged cover opens and closes easily and that, when closed, it sits squarely on the fire-bowl.
- Check that the grill adjustment levers operate smoothly and positively.
- Open and close all the air vents to ensure they are easy to move.
- Give it the 'wobble' test (see p. 6).

Wagon Barbecues

Wagon barbecues, because of their bulk and weight, are, for the most part, destined to spend their life on location – be it the patio or pool-side.

The name probably derives from the covered wagon, seen in countless Westerns. Like the prairie chuck-wagon, the wagon barbecue counterpart is mounted on, or is an integral part of, a four-wheeled base. (Two-wheeled versions are also available.) The rectangular chassis is available in a variety of materials including cast iron, cast aluminium, wrought iron, sheet metal and hardwood. The barbecue itself – charcoal, gas or electric – is usually made from cast iron or aluminium.

Some models are very elaborate – not perhaps conducive to making barbecuing an impromptu, outdoor adventure. In addition to the standard paraphernalia most have built-in storage space and ample working-surfaces for carving meat, etc. Wagons can be hooded or open but because they are likely to be permanently outside, the most practical units are the hooded weather-proof models.

Most wagons have extra large cooking capacities and are designed to cater for large parties. They certainly fit the bill when it comes to pool-side entertainment because with the built-in cupboard space usually provided, it is possible to have everything at hand with which to cook and serve the food.

One interesting new wagon barbecue was launched a couple of years ago by a British company. This model has a unique control system whereby the cooking grills (it has two, of the hinged, broiler type) can quickly be raised high above the fire-bed by operating a treadle. This device enables the chef to raise the meat well above flames caused by excessive fat and carry on cooking it, knowing that the food will not be ruined. Other features of this barbecue (which can be seen in the background of the photograph on p. 2) include a stainless steel tray for keeping cooked and part-cooked food warm, a full-length adjustable air vent (with ash tray under) and a large wooden work table. The barbecue can be used with either a normal-size spit for roasting chickens, or a jumbo spit for roasting lamb or sucking pig. Not featured in the photographs, but available as an optional extra, is a lid that converts the open barbecue to a smoker.

Check Points

- Can the barbecue be easily manoeuvred?
- If required, could the barbecue be easily packed down for end-of-season storage?
- Are the materials it is made from really weather-proof? If not, is a weather-proof cover available?

Universal Barbecues

The route into barbecuing for most people is via a small, fully portable model costing just a few pounds. The common tendency thereafter is to purchase a series of barbecues, each a little larger and a little bit more refined. The sequence for a good many barbecuers is to progress in a fairly logical manner from an hibachi or picnic barbecue to a brazier or hooded barbecue, then a covered barbecue (kettle or square) and finally perhaps a gas barbecue. Invariably the cheap basic models will have been either given or thrown away en route. The whole exercise could turn out to be quite costly, in terms of money spent and, to a certain extent, wasted.

A British company has now come up with a radical alternative – the world's first modular barbecue system, dubbed with the generic name 'Universal'. This is most appropriate because the Universal does provide the maximum number of alternatives in outdoor cooking, since it allows the user to add kits and accessories later to increase the barbecue's capacity and its range of cooking techniques.

The heart of the Universal system is a basic unit designed for table-top or picnic use. At the centre of the basic unit, and of the system itself, is a triangular column; on each side it has four brackets on which to hook the food grill, at a selected height above the charcoal fire, and a slot on which to clip the deep fire-bowl. The basic unit also has a couple of legs, for stability, and a wind-shield.

In addition to the basic unit, the system comprises various other models, all fully mobile, that range from a single fire-bowl unit to one with three fire-bowls. The latter comes complete with a domed lid enabling it to be used as a kettle barbecue. When thus used, two of the three fire-bowls are lined with aluminium foil (to make cleaning easier), and the remaining bowl is used to accommodate the fuel (see fig. 1).

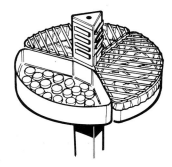

1　The Universal barbecue set up for indirect cooking (minus lid)

The meat is positioned over the empty bowls, thereby eliminating the problem, caused by fat dropping on to the fire, of excessive smoke or flare-ups. By using two or three fire-bowls one can vary the heat of each to suit different foods being cooked.

One of the models, complete with domed lid, is particularly clever, and unique in the world of barbecuing, in that it incorporates one gas-fired bowl and two charcoal-burning bowls in its three-bowl configuration. This gives the user a choice between the two cooking mediums, gas probably being the first choice for the cook who is in a hurry.

Those who wish at some stage to increase their barbecue's capacity can purchase various components. These include a kit to bring the basic unit up to waist height and extra fire-bowls. Having added one or two extra bowls to complete the circle (see fig. 1) they can then, if they wish, purchase a lid to make their barbecue suitable for indirect (kettle) cooking. Other options include a fire-bowl that has been converted to gas and a fire-bowl made in stainless steel with a slide-in gas burner under its base. The stainless steel bowl can also be used as a pan to prepare baked beans, boil fresh vegetables, heat soup and so on.

A rotisserie is available for spit-roasting which allows the owners of two- or three-bowl units to spit-roast a chicken or leg of lamb over one bowl while direct grilling steaks, etc., over another bowl. Another very handy accessory is used to keep cooked or part-cooked food warm, so greatly extending the barbecue's capacity. It consists of a rod which supports one or two food grills. The rod is located in the hole at the top of the central support column and can be adjusted up or down, or spun round.

Improvised Barbecues

Even if you own a barbecue, there is still the odd occasion when an improvised barbecue could prove useful – if your barbecue is too large to pack up and take to the beach, for example, or if you are catering for an unusually large number of guests. It is not difficult to make an improvised barbecue so long as you have (a) a grill to support the food; (b) a receptacle to contain the fire – and even this is not necessary for a barbecue on the beach.

Beach Barbecue

The beach barbecue is probably the most rudimentary of all – a grill and a box of matches are the only equipment needed. The ideal grill for a beach barbecue – large enough to cook steaks, burgers, chops or sausages for up to six people – is a piece of chicken wire approximately 24 × 14 inches (61 × 36 cm). The chicken wire can be taken to the beach rolled up in a couple of sheets of newspaper and, having been flattened out, doubled over to reduce the hole size and give extra rigidity. Twisting the cut edges of the wire together will help to keep the grill flat. Before placing food on the grill the first time it is used, the grill should be positioned over the hot coals for a few minutes in order to burn off the galvanized coating.

Select your barbecue site carefully, especially if the beach is a busy one – late in the evening you will probably have the beach pretty much to yourself. Exposed beaches can be breezy places so choosing a sheltered spot will help to conserve your fuel and allow your guests to encircle the fire. If there are no large rocks to shelter behind a canvas windbreak should suffice.

Having selected your spot, scoop out a hollow in the sand approximately 16 inches (41 cm) square and 4 inches (10 cm) deep. Position some large dry stones around the edge of the depression – pushing them in so as to leave a fairly level surface on which to support the grill. Leave some gaps between the stones and scoop away a shallow channel on the windward side so that there is a good draught at the base of the fire. Place a pile of driftwood between the stones and burn it down to hot embers – DO NOT START COOKING UNTIL THE FLAMES HAVE DIED DOWN.

Biscuit Tins, Buckets and Barrows

Several familiar domestic and garden objects lend themselves to becoming improvised barbecues. Biscuit tins or the large circular toffee or chocolate tins both make excellent improvised fire-bowls, although the barbecue will obviously be of limited scope. In order to create sufficient draught for the fire it will be necessary to punch holes an inch or so up from the base of the side wall and three or four in the base, too. Also to help the air circulate, place the tin on a couple of house bricks, leaving a gap between the bricks. Finding a suitable food grill should present no problems. An old grill-pan rack or cake rack will do, providing it is large enough to sit across the top of the tin. Don't use a grill which has widely spaced bars, as you could end up constantly retrieving blackened chipolatas or burgers from the charcoal fire!

An old steel bucket can also be used, but bear in mind that the fire-bed should be not much more than 5 inches (13 cm) from the grill. One way of achieving this would be to fill the bucket with pieces of broken brick to the appropriate level. Once again it will be necessary to punch or drill holes in the bottom and sides to aid a through draught. Periodically it will be necessary to empty the bucket in order to get rid of the accumulated ash and perhaps the top layer of bricks if they have become covered with grease. Do not use earth to fill the bucket as that would effectively prevent any movement of air up through the charcoal.

If, however, you use an old metal wheelbarrow, you can fill the barrow with earth to within 4–6 inches (10–15 cm) of the rim. Spread a layer of clean gravel (approximately ¼ inch, 6 mm, in diameter) over the earth to a depth of 1 inch (2·5 cm). Alternatively, spread a layer of vermiculite (obtainable in small bags from most barbecue stockists) over the earth. Because of the large open surface area of the barrow, coupled with the gravel which allows the air to pass under the charcoal, there should be little problem in getting the charcoal lit and keeping it burning. Should there be a problem in obtaining a grill large enough to straddle the wheelbarrow, it can be solved by positioning two, four or six bricks directly on the gravel to support one or even two smaller grills. If using two grills, support one of them on bricks laid flat and the other on bricks standing on edge. This will allow the chef to use two different heat intensities – especially useful when grilling steaks.

Oil-drum Barbecue

Using an old oil-drum to make a barbecue demands far greater DIY skills than the improvised barbecues above.

First you must find yourself an old 40 gallon drum – not easy perhaps, unless you reside in the far north of Scotland or on the outskirts of Dallas. Having located your drum, you will then have to enlist the services of someone – probably your local garage – who owns an oxyacetylene burner to get the drum cut into two equal halves lengthwise. You can now make the two halves into two open barbecues, give one half away, or use both halves to make one splendid barrel barbecue.

To make an open barbecue all that will be necessary is to construct some form of support for the drum-half to bring the barbecue up to a convenient working height. Probably the easiest to make would be two pairs of swivel legs securely linked together, which, when opened, form two Xs in which the drum-half sits. Whatever system is adopted it must provide a stable base for the barbecue. Holes should be punched in the lower half of the barbecue. In order to set the fire-bed at a height close enough to the food grill it will be necessary to fabricate a charcoal grate from expanded metal (with diamond-shaped holes) or steel reinforcing mesh. Finding a chrome-plated food grill large enough to cover the drum-half could be a problem; again, one could use expanded metal cut to size.

To make a barrel barbecue using both halves of the drum, you will have to join the halves with two or three strong hinges. Fit charcoal and food grills in one half as required for the open unit. The leg supports will need to be much stronger to take the extra weight and to remain stable when the upper half of the barbecue is hinged open. To lessen the strain on the hinges, it is a good idea to incorporate wire stays just long enough to allow the lid to open just past the vertical position.

In order to prevent the fire from being snuffed out it will be necessary to drill holes in the lid – three or four ½ inch (1 cm) holes grouped together will be adequate. Finally, you will have to fit a handle – preferably with a hardwood grip – to the hinged lid.

Plank Barbecue

For details see pp. 54–5.

Odds and Bods

The improvised barbecues that I have described show what can be done using makeshift materials and a bit of ingenuity. Many variations are possible. One talented friend of mine used a discarded galvanized water tank to construct a highly efficient gas barbecue; South Africans will tell you that the best *braai* is cooked on a ploughshare.

Permanent Structures

A sure sign of the barbecue's increasing popularity is the fact that a barbecue built in the back garden will be mentioned by estate agents in their sales blurb.

The best time to construct a permanent barbecue is when laying out a new patio – one can design the barbecue so that it blends in with the overall concept and one can also make use of any building materials which have been left over.

Before you start, you should decide exactly what you want.

How Much Cooking Capacity?

The cost of a permanent barbecue – unlike a portable one – will not vary much with size. Bearing this in mind, and the fact that the barbecue will also make an excellent incinerator (having removed the grills, etc.) for burning garden rubbish, it is better to err on the side of making it slightly larger than you think you need. If you intend to buy one of the DIY barbecue kits (see pp. 20–21) or to use grills from a defunct cooker or refrigerator this will determine the size of the grill area. As a rough guide allow approximately 20 square inches (129 cm^2) per person when calculating the grill area required.

What Cooking Techniques?

Will you want to use your barbecue for spit-roasting as well as grilling? If so, how much meat would be spit-roasted at one time. The answer will determine whether you need a heavy-duty spit, with motor to match, or one of the standard spit assemblies which can be bought in most garden centres and stores.

If you intend to barbecue whole joints, even perhaps to bake bread, this will entail making a fairly close-fitting cover. Details are given on p. 62 of how to make a simple cover using wire and aluminium foil. The alternative is to make, or have made, a sheet-metal cover or to ask your local stockists if they can sell you the lid from a ready-made kettle barbecue.

If you want to use a wok a great deal, it would be better to make your barbecue round. (It is possible to buy circular food and charcoal grills.) Woks over 24 inches (61 cm) in diameter can be purchased from some barbecue stockists; small woks are readily available from most department and hardware stores.

You may also want to have a griddle (hot-plate) for frying burgers, eggs and bacon, and pancakes. This is particularly useful for breakfast or brunch. The hot-plate, usually made of cast iron or cast aluminium, can be fitted per-

Spicy lamb kebabs (p. 86), kidney and sausage kebabs (p. 85), cumgingon lamb kebabs (p. 83), Neville's mushroom and scallop kebabs (p. 106).

manently next to the wire food grill or it can be kept separately for heating on top of the food grill.

Some Ideas on Design

How many extras you build into your permanent barbecue will depend on how much you intend to use it, but don't get too carried away by enthusiasm for extra refinements – warming ovens, fuel stores, work-tops and so on – after all, it is a barbecue that you are building not an imitation of your kitchen lay-out!

A Semi-permanent Barbecue

Figure 2 shows a design for a semi-permanent barbecue, shaped like a well and constructed from layers of unmortared bricks. The advantages of this type of barbecue are threefold: the construction work requires no more skill than a child making something from building blocks because no mortar is required; the barbecue can easily be moved to another spot should your first choice of location prove unsatisfactory (see pp. 19–20 for advice on where to locate your barbecue); and, if you wish, the barbecue can be dismantled at the end of the summer and the metal components stored until the following spring. All the components, excluding the bricks (approximately a hundred are required) are available in kit form from most barbecue stockists (see pp. 20–21). If possible, use over-burnt bricks which are less liable to crumble when subjected to intense heat.

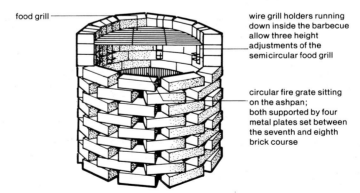

food grill

wire grill holders running down inside the barbecue allow three height adjustments of the semicircular food grill

circular fire grate sitting on the ashpan; both supported by four metal plates set between the seventh and eighth brick course

2   Free-standing 'wishing-well' shaped barbecue, constructed from loose house bricks. It will take approximately 30 minutes to build

A Built-in Barbecue

Figure 3 shows a barbecue that is relatively simple to build and easy to maintain. The ironmongery you use will dictate the size of the structure. You

Grilled sardines (p. 110), red mullet grilled with fennel (p. 106), barbecued salmon steaks (p. 109), spicy grilled prawns (p. 74), prawns with a hint of mint (p. 74).

should be able to get it from your local barbecue stockist, but you could retrieve roasting pans and chrome-plated grills from a discarded cooker. You can also use the wire shelves from an old refrigerator for the food grills, but they are rather flimsy. If you do, try to obtain some spares, all the same size of course, for replacements. It is a good idea, if you can, to fit two or three grills at different levels. This increases the barbecue's capacity and allows the chef to vary the heat level – using the lowest grill to sear meat and then moving it further away from the heat to finish cooking more slowly. The doors which fit below the grate, allowing the ashes to be emptied, can be bought separately.

If you are using a commercial barbecue kit for the ironmongery, it will include a rotisserie unit – spit, spit-support brackets, meat tines and battery-

3 Basic permanent installation incorporating good working-surfaces for the chef, handily placed cupboards and shelf space, and adjacent seating for guests. The small door situated below the charcoal grill permits ash removal and draught control

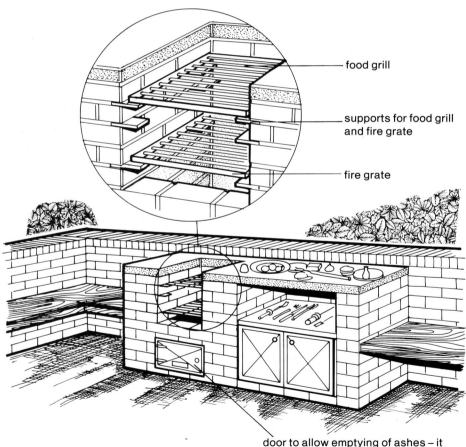

food grill

supports for food grill and fire grate

fire grate

door to allow emptying of ashes – it includes an adjustable ventilation slot

operated motor. A spit-roast assembly can also be bought separately, but you may have to manufacture your own spit-support brackets from thick galvanized fencing wire or ³⁄₁₆ inch (4 mm) mild steel plate.

Barbecuing is very social, so rather than have one person preparing salads and so on in the kitchen while the food is being cooked in the garden, the perfect design should include a suitable work-surface near but not too close to the barbecue itself. The installation of a sink and tap would make the barbecue area completely self-contained; the simple push-fit plumbing systems now available are well within the capability of the average DIY enthusiast.

Installing an underground cable to provide a power source for an outdoor light is well worth contemplating but that is one job to be tackled by a professional.

What Materials to Use?

The proportion and design of your permanent barbecue should be in harmony with your house, patio and garden, and you will achieve this more easily if you use the same or matching building materials. In fact, there is a lot to be said for incorporating the barbecue into a low patio or garden wall so that it blends into its surroundings.

Most permanent barbecues are constructed from bricks or reconstituted stone because natural stone is usually very expensive and is also quite difficult to work. When used properly a natural stone structure can look stunning, but on the other hand it can look incongruous in the wrong setting. Many varieties of natural stone – other than those which are volcanic in origin – are liable to crack or even shatter when subjected to the heat of a charcoal fire. Concrete building blocks and ordinary bricks are also liable to crack, and it is therefore best to line the inside walls and base of the barbecue with firebricks or – considerably cheaper – a good quality house brick that has been left in the baking oven too long. You may be able to find some over-burnt bricks in the yard of your local builders' merchant or at a brickworks.

Where to Locate It?

Great care should be exercised when deciding where to locate the barbecue if it is to be a permanent structure.

Common sense will tell you where not to site it – slap bang in front of your french windows, for example. It is worth experimenting with a portable barbecue to try out possible sites. This will help to determine if there are any problems in getting the charcoal alight and controlling the fire thereafter in the position you have chosen. Barbecues that are free-standing can incorporate air vents at the base, on all sides if necessary, to allow for the vagaries of the wind. Barbecues built into a patio wall will normally have an air vent at the front only but if the structure projects forward from the line of the wall by at least 12 inches (30 cm) this will allow three air vents to be built in – one each side and one on the front. It is important to arrange that all the vents can be individually opened and closed by means of a shutter, so that those vents not facing into the wind can be fully or partly closed to improve the through draught.

Some Constructive Comments

Like any other stone or brick structure, a permanent barbecue will require a proper foundation. If the spot selected is level and stable, and the earth well compacted (it should certainly not have been dug over during the previous ten years or so) then it should be necessary to excavate the area only to a depth of approximately 10 inches (25 cm). The bottom 6 inches (15 cm) of the excavation should be laid with hardcore and then covered to ground level with a mix of one part ordinary Portland cement, three parts damp sand and six parts gravel. Barbecues built on heavy clay (which is liable to shrink in hot weather and expand in wet conditions) or friable soil will require deeper foundations. Where a particularly heavy structure is contemplated one should lay steel reinforcing mesh after half the concrete has been poured; the remaining concrete should be tamped down to ensure that the two layers bind well together.

It is a good idea to pave the area round the barbecue if it is not on the patio; paving slabs can form an attractive feature of the barbecue design, and a textured surface reduces the risk of slipping. There is now a very wide choice of paving slabs to choose from, some of which are similar in appearance, but not in shape, to York stone. Standard 'local authority' paving is cheap, but its drab grey colour may not blend too well with the rest of the barbecue. They are also extremely heavy.

Practical advice on the design and construction of a patio, which should prove useful when building a barbecue, too, is given in the booklets available from most large manufacturers of pre-cast slabs and building materials. One company even sells a kit of reconstituted stone blocks together with full building instructions; a useful feature of their kit is that it contains some wider blocks that, set into the walls of the barbecue, jut out to form supports for the food grill, fire-tray or grate.

DIY Barbecue Kits

During the past few years there has been a marked increase in the number of people interested in building a permanent barbecue in their garden or back yard (see above). In order to meet this demand some companies now offer a range of barbecue kits. The standard kit normally includes a chrome-plated grill, a charcoal grid, grill supports, a metal tray, a wind-shield and a rotisserie unit. Grill sizes for the rectangular versions vary from around 15 × 17 inches (38 × 43 cm) to 43 × 17 inches (109 × 43 cm). Most kits are designed to be used in a rectangular brick-built structure which may require anything from around ninety to over 130 bricks to complete. One recent addition to the range of kits available caters for those people who wish to install a gas-burning unit.

Fire-pit Barbecues

Cooking meat underground has been practised for many years past in North America – indeed, they have refined the technique to the point where some barbecue pits are constructed with the same type of building materials and attention to detail that is generally employed for permanent above-ground installations.

Steam Cooking

Although referred to as a barbecuing technique any food (meat or fish) cooked in this manner is not broiled, since it does not come in direct contact with naked heat. In fact, because the food is completely wrapped in layers of foil or closely woven white cloth, the cooking method is more akin to that of a pressure cooker than a barbecue. Another important difference between barbecuing above ground and cooking underground is that when the fire-pit is sealed there is no opportunity to have a peek at how the food is cooking – this would be tantamount to opening the oven door halfway through baking a soufflé! It can be difficult to gauge cooking times because of the many variables involved. Constant practice will help, but there will never be any guarantee that the meat is not either over- or under-cooked. As a very rough guide a joint of meat weighing between 5 and 10 lb (2·3–4·5 kg) will take approximately 5 hours to cook while a 20 lb (9 kg) piece will take about twice as long. Larger pieces, i.e. hindquarters, will take proportionally less time to cook, but it is advisable to stick to joints which weigh not more than 20 lb (9 kg) to make serving and handling the meat easier.

The width and length of the fire-pit will be determined by the size of the food packages to be accommodated spread out in a single layer with a 2–3 inch (5–7·5 cm) gap between the packages and the sides of the pit. It will be easier to remove the food from the fire-pit if the width is restricted to no more than 3 ft (0·9 m). The length is determined by the amount of food to be contained within the recommended maximum width. The depth of the fire-pit can be worked out by adding together the following measurements:

(a) the depth of the bed of hot coals – anywhere from 6 to 24 inches (15 to 61 cm) depending upon the amount of food to be cooked and the type, i.e. a 5–10 lb (2·3–4·5 kg) joint will need approximately 12 inches (30 cm) of hot coals, while a large fish (sea bass or salmon) will take only 50–60 minutes over a bed of hot coals approximately 6 inches (15 cm) deep;

(b) the thickness of the largest joint; and

(c) the layer of earth or sand – usually about 12 inches (30 cm) deep. For most standard pits the depth will therefore probably be in the order of 36–42 inches (91–107 cm).

Having dug out the requisite amount of soil, line the bottom with dry, preferably smooth, large stones or fire-bricks; alternatively, use over-burnt house bricks. If there are sufficient stones or bricks left over these can be used to build up side walls high enough to match the depth of the bed of coals.

Having dug and prepared the pit the next step is to create a bed of hot coals. The best woods to use are hardwoods such as oak, elm, beech, apple and walnut (if you are lucky). The wood should be dry and preferably in billets 3–4 inches (7·5–10 cm) thick. In order to create a fire-bed approximately 6 inches (15 cm) deep one would have to burn down a layer of wood covering the same area to a depth of about 3 ft (91 cm). It is important that all the wood should be thoroughly charred – almost charcoal – before the meat is placed in position.

The meat should be securely wrapped in two or three layers of white cloth or heavy-duty aluminium foil and then in one, or preferably two, layers of burlap. The complete package should be tied securely with wire and well doused with water.

The next step is to lay the packages of meat on top of the hot coals – if the fire-pit has been dug into the beach it is a good idea to spread a layer of heated sand, taken from around the base of the pit, over the hot coals to a depth of approximately 1 inch (2·5 cm).

When the packages of meat are in place, they should be quickly covered with earth or sand, before they start to dry out and scorch. The really organized chef will have a pre-cut piece of corrugated iron (with the galvanizing previously burnt off) or a piece of sheet metal to place on top of the meat packages before shovelling on the covering layer. Particular attention should be paid to ensure that no steam or smoke escapes through the layer of earth or sand and regular inspections of the fire-pit should be undertaken to check that no steam is in fact seeping out. If the earth is very dry and crumbly it is a good idea to wet the surface in order to produce a 'glazed' seal.

Meat cooked by this method will be very succulent but as the surfaces have not been seared the meat will tend to dry out quite rapidly when exposed to the air.

Roasting

Another type of pit barbecue which allows the meat to be roasted rather than steam-cooked is in the form of a pit completely lined with fire-bricks. There are two important differences to the type discussed above. First, the space is enclosed and the heat retained, either with a pair of hinged lids manufactured from ¼ inch (6 mm) steel plate or a number of planks butted closely together and then covered with a large sheet of canvas. The edges of the doors or the canvas will need to be sealed with a layer of earth. Second, the joints of meat, which should be left unwrapped, are suspended above the hot coals in a stretcher made from a piece of flexible heavy-duty wire mesh which is securely bolted to two 1½ inch (38 mm) steel pipes. The steel pipes should be long enough to rest in half-round recesses on the pit walls and the base of the wire basket should be some 18–24 inches (46–61 cm) above the bed of hot coals. Dimensions will of course vary according to the amount of meat to be barbecued, but a pit approximately 6 × 4 ft (183 × 122 cm), and 5 ft (152 cm) deep, in which a wire basket some 24 inches (61 cm) wide is hung, should be able to accommodate joints of meat to feed 200–250 people.

Pit barbecues are very similar to mini-elephant traps so do not leave them uncovered when not in use. People might fall into them, and they will eventually fill with rainwater.

Gas Barbecues

The big advantage of gas-fired barbecues is that they are ready for use only 10 minutes after they have been lit, whereas a charcoal-burning barbecue has to heat up for 45 minutes. Another plus is the variable heat control. In North America gas-fired barbecues are now 20 per cent, by volume, of all barbecue sales. Although some gas barbecues can be adapted fairly easily to run off natural gas very few are in fact plumbed in to the natural gas supply. The main advantage of liquefied petroleum gas (LPG) over mains gas is that it comes in containers which are easily stored and can be used anywhere. The majority of gas barbecues now sold in the UK are imported from the USA or Canada and are designed to be used with propane gas. Propane gas (supplied in cylinders painted red or orange) has one major advantage over butane gas (supplied in cylinders painted blue): it has a lower freezing temperature, thus enabling the barbecue to be used, if required, throughout the winter months without too much deterioration in performance. People living at higher altitudes will also find they achieve better results from their barbecue when using propane. Probably because propane cylinders are less widely available in the UK, most people here use butane gas for their barbecues, even though the results, if the barbecue is designed for propane, are somewhat less satisfactory.

The fuel element in a gas barbecue is lava rock or, in some instances, man-made ceramic blocks or small nuggets. When exposed to a gas flame the rock emits a radiant heat, although there is no discernible change in its appearance. (It does not glow.) With both gas and charcoal-burning barbecues the food is cooked by radiant heat, not by contact with the flames. Indeed, when licked by flames from a charcoal or wood fire meat will quickly become charred on the outside while remaining somewhat raw on the inside – a highly undesirable combination for most meats but especially so for pork sausages and chicken.

There will always be traditionalists who pooh-pooh the idea that food can be barbecued over anything other than charcoal. No amount of argument will persuade them otherwise – even when reminded that charcoal is both odourless and flavourless. The magical 'outdoor' flavour in barbecued meat is imparted to the meat by the smoke produced when the savoury juices hit the hot coals – or in the case of a gas barbecue, the hot lava rock.

Most gas barbecues on sale are, because of their bulk, destined to spend their lives on the patio; there are, however, several fully portable models available.

Tips

- Having purchased your gas barbecue the first thing to do is to sit down and read carefully all the information supplied by the manufacturer.

- After it has been used a few times the lava rocks will probably become grease-laden. They can be cleaned by subjecting them to high heat for approximately 10 minutes just after a cooking session; this is even more effective if you cover the rocks with two or three layers of heavy-duty aluminium foil and keep the barbecue lid in the closed position. Alternatively, boil the rocks in water to which a small amount of detergent has been added – it will of course be necessary to allow the rocks to dry thoroughly before reusing them.

- Gas cylinders should always be treated with respect. Never store or carry them upside down because this may result in the control valve being damaged, and leaks can be dangerous. Always use a cylinder upright; if you use it horizontally, liquid fuel could get into the supply pipes, with serious results. Keep the cylinders away from heat.
  NEVER store cylinders below ground level, e.g. in cellars, because if there is a leak the gas, being heavier than air, will collect at a low level and become dangerous in the presence of flame or a spark.

- Make sure you have the means of lighting the gas *before* turning on the supply.

- Never start up the lighting procedure with the lid of the barbecue *in situ*.

- LPG has a distinct smell to help in the detection of leaks; NEVER look for a leak with a naked light!
- When changing a cylinder make sure the appliance is switched OFF.

Electric Barbecues

Electric barbecues are similar to gas in that they use long-lasting volcanic rock to absorb and then radiate the heat; and both are ready for action within 10 minutes of starting up. However, electric barbecues are irrevocably tied to the power supply – the house.

Electric barbecues became available on the North American market many years ago but have made relatively little impact, although modest quantities, very modest when compared to gas barbecues, continue to be sold each year. There is no doubt, however, that some people prefer electricity to gas as a cooking medium. A British company has recently introduced its own version of an electric barbecue. Although rather expensive, when compared to charcoal-burning barbecues with similar grill areas, electric barbecues have a decided edge when it comes to running costs. They have variable heat control but, unlike gas and charcoal-burning barbecues, they are at present limited to direct grilling of fast-cooking meat and fish, and suitable vegetables (see pp. 48–9).

Accessories and Tools

In keeping perhaps with the relaxed nature of barbecuing, some of the gadgets available tend to be rather frivolous, but some should certainly form part of any barbecue starter kit. This section should help you sort out what you need.

For the Barbecue and the Fire

Cleaning Materials

The special wire brushes, complete with a metal scraper, that are now readily available from most stockists, seem a good idea, but after just a few encounters with a grease-encrusted barbecue food grill the fine wire bristles tend to become completely clogged up. The chrome plating that covers most grills is rather thin and one should certainly avoid using a stiff wire brush. I find that rubbing a crumpled piece of aluminium foil over the grill bars (both sides) before the fat has had time to congeal will remove much of the grease and most of the rest can then be wiped off with kitchen paper. Leaving your food grill covered in a thin film of grease will help to keep rust at bay. The grill must then be 'cauterized' over hot coals and wiped once again with kitchen paper before barbecuing the next batch of food.

If you use the barbecue regularly, say once or more a week, it is a good idea to spring clean the barbecue halfway through the season; always clean it thoroughly at the end of the season. To deal with the accumulation of grease it will be necessary to use one of the standard proprietary oven cleaners or the aerosol spray cleaner now available at most barbecue stockists. In addition to cleaning the barbecue itself, complete the job by washing all the 'iron-mongery' – skewers, spit assembly, tools, and so on – in hot soapy water. Dry them well and protect the chrome-work of the accessories and tools with a thin coating of vaseline or light oil. This is particularly important if you plan to store the items in the garage or an outhouse.

Fire-base

Many picnic and brazier barbecues have fire-bowls that do not incorporate adjustable air vents or perforations of any kind. To aid charcoal ignition when using them it is a good idea to lay the charcoal on a granular base (see pp. 41–2).

Vermiculite fire-base is available in small bags from most barbecue stockists or in large sacks from builders' merchants. The only other base which will allow the free passage of air underneath the charcoal is dry, clean river gravel. Gravel should be pea-sized (approximately a quarter of an inch, 6 mm in diameter).

Fire Starters

See pp. 39–40.

Foil

A tremendous boon for the barbecue chef, next in importance perhaps to a good pair of tongs, is extra-thick aluminium foil. I find the 18 inch (46 cm) width ideal for lining fire-bowls and making up drip trays (see p. 61). A double layer of extra-thick foil laid on the food grill makes a useful hot-plate and foil lapped on to a wire frame makes an excellent improvised barbecue cover (see p. 62).

Fuel

See pp. 36–8.

Illumination

As most barbecue parties are held in the evening, a reasonable degree of lighting is therefore necessary, both to let the guests see where they are treading and to let the chef see what he or she is doing. If the barbecue is reasonably close to the house it should not be too difficult to rig up a temporary overhead cable to provide light. If the barbecue is built in, and well used, it would certainly be worth installing a permanent light powered from the mains via an underground cable. (This is a job for a qualified electrician.)

The area around the barbecue could be lit more softly and romantically by using one or more of the excellent garden lighting kits with their multi-coloured bulbs. The coloured bulb (or bulbs) nearest the chef could be replaced with an ordinary bulb to give enough light to work by.

Hurricane lights can also be used for direct light. Background lights (which do little more than heighten the festive mood) are now available in most garden centres and stores; they include wax flares, candles in glass or plastic 'cups' (mounted on canes) and long-burning wicks fuelled by paraffin in a container incorporated into a long piece of thick cane.

Tongs

When spit-roasting chicken and other joints it is useful to have a pair of tongs with extra long handles for rearranging the hot charcoal; this task can be most uncomfortable even when wearing thick leather gauntlets so the further one's hand is away from the heat the better. 'Fire-tending' tool sets, which normally include a small rake as well as a pair of long-handled tongs, are available in a few specialist establishments.

For the Chef

Basting Brush

A good basting brush is made from pure bristle. Brushes made from nylon or plastic are not recommended for basting food on a barbecue. It's a good idea to keep one brush for applying fats (oil and butter) and another for applying sauces and seasoning. Tube basters are also quite useful but they tend to be rather fiddly to wash after use.

Boards

Every barbecue chef should have a home-made, oversize, hardwood board; carving boards borrowed from the kitchen are usually too small to cope with the amount of carving and cutting usually required. Alternatively, handsome laminated carving boards can be bought in most department stores.

Foil

Heavy-duty aluminium foil is required at every stage of barbecuing. I find the 30 cm width perfect for wrapping and covering food. Vegetables wrapped loosely, yet securely, in a foil pack will be steam-cooked, while potatoes and onions wrapped tightly in a couple of layers of foil can be baked among hot coals. Extra-thick foil is indispensable for anyone making or using a pit barbecue (see pp. 21–3).

Protruding bits of food like chicken or turkey wings and leg knuckles, rib ends on a crown roast or guard of honour and fish tails can be protected from burning and charring with a foil cover.

Foilware

Small foilware dishes are excellent for keeping sauces warm and the larger ones are useful for marinating food or using as a drip pan. Foilware plates, serving dishes and so on make excellent barbecue-to-table cookware.

Forks

Like all tools used for barbecue cooking, forks should be long-handled; the grip should be comfortable and preferably made from wood.

Gloves and Apron

In order to keep clothes clean and hands free from blisters the chef will need adequate protection. First and foremost a pair of good-quality oven gloves are required, preferably gauntlets that cover the wrists and lower forearm completely. Unfortunately, most so-called barbecue gloves are barely adequate for protecting one's hands from anything hotter than a lighted match!

For comfort and utility I prefer a sturdy cloth apron, long enough to cover my knees, with a couple of wide pockets in the front.

Kitchen Paper

A roll of absorbent paper towelling, slung from the waist by a piece of string, is invaluable. It's great for mopping up (and mopping brows), wrapping smelly garbage, wiping greasy hands or simply wrapping round a hot sausage before handing it to a hungry guest.

Knives

When you have produced a superb roast, you will not want to ruin the effect by using a poor-quality carving knife.

You will need the same array of sharp paring, slicing and carving knives that you would normally use in the kitchen. If anything, their quality should be rather higher, to overcome the occasional hazards of working outdoors on less convenient surfaces.

Pans

A heavy saucepan, filled with vast quantities of hot food, needs careful handling and should have long two-handed handles.

Skewers

There is nothing quite as frustrating as turning a meat-laden skewer only to find that, while the skewer itself has rotated, the food has stayed still. Skewers should therefore have flat blades, about ¼ inch (6 mm) wide, and a sturdy handle with, ideally, a hand-shield. Skewers are usually made from stainless steel although many of those imported from the Far East (some with very decorative handles) are of ordinary steel and are liable to rust if not looked after properly.

Skewers made from hardwood or bamboo slivers are intended for grilling saté.

If your barbecue has a spit unit, you can purchase a shish-kebab set to fit on to the spit-rod. The set comprises two round plates accommodating four skewers.

Spit, Spit Motor, Balance Weights

The 'spit' on some small cheap barbecues may be supported on such a shallow wind-shield that anything other than a rather immature pigeon would be in danger of constantly brushing the charcoal lying in the fire-bowl below! Even on some of the larger and more expensive barbecues the spit and its motor (if supplied) tend to be rather on the flimsy side. Spit-rods should be capable of supporting 6–7 lb (2·7–3·2 kg) of food (roughly the weight of two average-sized chickens) without deflecting unduly. The thumb-screws securing the tines to the spit-rod should be strong enough to be tightened firmly without the threads stripping. The spit motor, usually battery driven, has a lot of fairly heavy work to do – a leg of lamb will need to be turned constantly for a period of up to three hours. American electrically driven motors can be difficult to find, but they are capable of turning up to 20 lb (9 kg) of meat at around 4 r.p.m. indefinitely. Clockwork, spit motors are available with some barbecues but although they perform well they are in constant need of rewinding. A failed motor, be it electrically driven or clockwork, wreaks havoc with the meat on the spit – if unattended, the meat will quickly char on one side and remain semi-raw on the other.

Balancing the meat on the spit is very important (see p. 50) but can prove difficult with irregular-shaped joints, particularly if the meat changes its centre of gravity during cooking due to the fat falling away. One can overcome the problem by using adjustable balance weights; tracking down a set may prove somewhat difficult, however.

Sprinkler

Even the most experienced barbecue chef sometimes has to cope with the odd flare-up – usually caused by a combination of excessive heat and excessively fatty food. Dousing or subduing the unwanted flames on an open barbecue should be tackled carefully so as not to ruin either the hot bed of coals or the barbecue itself; too much water, too quickly applied, should be avoided at all costs. The best type of sprinkler to use is the small hand-spray used for spraying indoor plants; it easily adjusts from a narrow stream of water to a very fine spray. Remove the food from above the flames and direct a fine mist-spray at the seat of the flames until they start to subside.

Strong String

A ball of good twine should always be kept handy for trussing birds and roasts of irregular shape and anchoring meat and fish on the spit and tines.

Thermometer

Meat thermometers are very useful for taking most of the guesswork out of cooking very large joints. Most have either a round clock-type face with a

4   A large joint of beef ready for spit-roasting, with meat thermometer inserted

moving hand that broadly tells you if the meat is rare or well done, or a flat arrow-shaped face with a column of mercury.

The point of the thermometer should be pushed into the centre of the joint (or large fish), but check that it does not rest against a bone or, if spit-roasting, the metal spit. A false reading will also occur if the tip of the thermometer rests in a pocket of fat.

Tongs

A pair of long-handled tongs is indispensable. Tongs can vary enormously in price and efficiency, with a good pair costing perhaps ten times as much as the cheapest. They should have long handles with comfortable wooden grips to make it easy to manipulate small pieces of food, on to, off and around the grill.

One should not have to apply great pressure to close the tongs – they should, ideally, feel and operate like a natural extension of the hand. A problem with many cheap tongs is that the blades tend to become crossed and twisted when handling small sausages and other items. Tongs that have sharp gripping teeth are not suitable for handling grilled meat, steak in particular, because the meat, when pierced, will lose some of its natural juices.

Waste Bin

Barbecue parties comprising more than a dozen or so guests will create a fair amount of debris if the tableware is disposable. Adequate provision should therefore be made for the disposal of napkins, plates and leftovers.

Wire Broiler

Reminiscent of the days before the advent of detergents and washing powders, when a hinged wire basket was used to beat soap into the wash, are the wire broilers with long handles used in barbecuing flat foods (fig. 5). It is now possible to buy broilers designed to accommodate hamburgers, steaks and fish in varying quantities. They allow a quantity of hot food to be handled

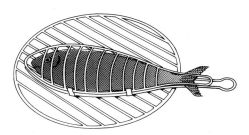

5   Hinged wire broiler for fish

simultaneously; the fish broiler overcomes the problem of turning a part-cooked fish without it starting to break up. Most fish broilers are suitable for, say, a trout weighing up to 10 oz (275 g) but one can buy broilers that will accommodate three fish of this size; very large broilers that will handle a fish weighing several pounds. There is even a version which will accommodate a dozen sardines.

A variation on the broiler is the flat or cylindrical-shaped wire basket which is designed for clamping to a spit-rod. The cylindrical type allows chicken pieces, etc., to tumble freely; the flat basket is used to clamp steaks, chops, etc., into position.

For Serving

Bowls and Baskets

Wooden, metal or plastic bowls will be required for things like salads and sauces. A basket is perhaps the nicest way to cope with bread rolls, slices of French bread or toast.

Coffee-pot

The heat from the barbecue (charcoal or gas) can be used to make pots of coffee; alternatively, the coffee can be made indoors and brought to the party area in a thermos jug.

Cups

A barbecue party, unless it is a small sit-down, rather formal, affair, is not the place to bring out one's best china. Paper cups or the slightly more expensive plastic-coated cups can be used for most drinks.

Cutlery

Unless you are serving prime steak, it will be necessary to provide really sharp steak knives – sawing through meat while balancing a plastic plate on one's lap can prove to be a messy business. Apart from steak knives, cutlery can be kept to a minimum, as much of what is cooked at barbecue parties is finger food. Cheap plastic cutlery can be thrown away after use but the more rugged type is worth washing and keeping for another day.

Accessories and Tools

Foilware

See p. 28.

Ice Bucket

Keeping the wine, or for that matter the lemonade, cool is important in making the party a success. This is especially so when the sun is beating down or the evening is warm and muggy. Use an ice-bucket – or simply a bucket with ice in.

Openers

A useful gadget is the one that does duty as bottle opener, can opener and corkscrew. (A barbecue that is frequently taken on picnics should have one permanently tied to it!)

Paper Napkins

Eating barbecued food using one's fingers can be a messy business so a good supply of paper napkins is essential. The napkins should be strong and absorbent. Pieces of kitchen paper will do, but the small gaily coloured flimsies which take neither grease nor water will not.

Pepper, Salt, Herbs and Seasoning

A large and sturdy set comprising a pepper-mill and salt shaker are musts, plus a selection of herbs and seasonings for the chef to use.

Plates

As cups. Paper plates will do, but it's worth investing in a stock of the 'unbreakable' plastic type. Balancing a glass of wine while eating can be tricky, and it might be a good idea to buy some of the new party plates which allow you to anchor the wine glass to the plate with your thumb. The original idea was probably based on the artist's palette.

Sauces

It is not a bad idea to have a small selection of bottled sauces on hand. If you want to serve home-made sauces hot from the grill, a fireproof dish will be necessary.

33

The Barbecue

Serving Spoons

You will need at least one set of serving spoons for the salad; you may also need serving spoons for sauces (long-handled if they are to be served direct from the barbecue) or vegetables.

Trolley

A wheeled trolley or serving centre, such as the one illustrated, makes serving easier.

6   Mobile serving centre incorporating large wooden working-surface and three sliding drawers for holding salads, condiments, ice, etc.

Just in Case

Bug-repellents

The food and lights of a summer evening barbecue will attract insects; an occasional squirt from a bug-repellent spray will deal with most of them. (Be careful to avoid uncovered food!)

One can now buy insect-repellent citronella candles (citronella is a fragrant grass which yields an oil used in perfumery) that will burn for many hours. Also available are insect-repellent garden torches which work on the same principle.

Those people who live in low-lying areas where biting insects abound can do little about it, apart perhaps from buying one of the new outdoor flying-insect killers like those one sees in butchers' shops. Although rather expensive, it is claimed that electrically powered units effectively rid large areas (up to two acres) from the dreaded gnat and its kindred.

Burn Lotion

One is unlikely to avoid the odd burn or blister from time to time. Various lotions, ointments and sprays can be obtained from the chemist to counteract the worst effects; or you can use the old-fashioned remedy of linseed oil and lime water.

First-aid Kit

Apart from the odd bug and the odd burn, your barbecue party should be no more accident prone than any indoor gathering, but it does make sense when picnicking away from home to carry a small first-aid kit. The minimum contents should be a lotion or spray for burns, plasters, aspirins and antiseptic.

2 Fuel, Firelighters and Firemanship

Fuel

Experienced chefs will tell you that the success, or otherwise, of any cook-out will hang on the quality of the charcoal being used as well as on the building up of a good fire (see pp. 41–2). It is annoying therefore that charcoal sold for barbecuing can vary enormously in quality. Before blaming yourself, or your equipment, for an unsatisfactory performance, consider whether the charcoal used was up to scratch. If in doubt, try another brand next time and, if necessary, keep doing so until you find one that is relatively easy to get started, gives off a consistently high heat and is long burning.

Charcoal

Charcoal burning has been practised as a skilled craft from as early as 4000 BC in central Africa. Charcoal-burners' conical huts (made of a wooden frame covered in sacking and turf) were a familiar sight in the Weald of Kent and Sussex for hundreds of years. Charcoal-burners were nomadic craftsmen who moved about the countryside setting up their camps and kilns wherever the wood was available.

Making charcoal in those days was a highly skilled and laborious business. The wood was stacked to make a kiln, which was then covered with thatch and earth so as to exclude air. Once it was lit it had to be watched day and night for up to a week to ensure that it remained airtight and the burning process was kept under control. Charcoal was in such great demand during the Tudor and Elizabethan period to fuel the hundred or so ironworks located throughout Kent and Sussex that statutes were eventually passed for the preservation of the English woods. Demand for charcoal had diminished by the beginning of the nineteenth century; the last production of iron by means of charcoal took place in Sussex in 1825.

Charcoal for barbecuing is available in two forms: as lumpwood or in uniformly shaped briquettes.

Lumpwood Charcoal

Charcoal straight from the kiln comes in lumps of varying sizes – hence the name – which are then broken up into graded pieces suitable for a barbecue. Good-quality lumpwood charcoal should be completely dry and feel light. There should be a minimum of dust and very small pieces lying in the bottom of the bag.

The best-quality lumpwood charcoal will be made from hardwoods, but it is not uncommon for softwoods to be mixed in as well. Charcoal is not particularly cheap and you can understand why when you are told that it takes approximately 6 tons of green wood to make 1 ton of charcoal.

Charcoal Briquettes

All briquettes are made from pulverized materials – whether 100-per-cent hardwood char, or a mixture of hardwood and mineral carbons that have been bound together with starch (sometimes other 'gluing' substances are used). Most pre-formed charcoal is pillow-shaped but the main British manufacturer produces rod-shaped briquettes.

Charcoal in briquette form is recommended for two reasons:
(a) the briquettes burn for about twice as long as lumpwood charcoal – more or less depending upon the quality and constituents of the briquette. This means that, since the selling prices for briquette and lumpwood charcoal are at present very similar, using briquettes is considerably cheaper. Also, a longer cooking session can be undertaken without the need to add further charcoal to the fire;
(b) being of uniform size and consistency, briquettes produce a uniform heat without the nuisance – sometimes experienced with lumpwood containing the odd piece of resinous softwood – of sparks flying out.

The best-quality charcoal briquettes are made from dense hardwoods with a low resin content, such as oak, beech and birch. The 'char' content of the top-quality briquettes can be as high as 97 per cent with the remaining 3 per cent being a starch binder. Briquettes of this quality are easy to light and burn very hot and for a long time. Some brands of charcoal briquettes contain a much higher mineral content than others – usually lignite or anthracite – with which to supplement the hardwood content. In fact the hardwood content of a briquette can vary from just over 50 per cent up to 97 per cent. Some briquettes also contain an inordinate amount of inert filling material which provides no heat but is presumably added to reduce product costs. Should you find that the heat emitted from your charcoal fire appears less than you would expect, try another brand next time. It can be a false economy to buy the cheapest.

Because of its high density, a briquette is not as easy to ignite as a piece of lumpwood charcoal. There are some brands of briquettes available which are specially treated with an ignition agent to make lighting easier. These products tend, however, to be considerably more expensive than the un-treated briquettes and they should never be used to stoke up an existing fire over which food is cooking, as the fumes given off will probably ruin the food.

Charcoal, when burning, gives off carbon monoxide gas. You should therefore NEVER cook with it in a confined space, though you could use a small barbecue in a fireplace recess where there is a good upward draught created by leaving a door or window open.

REMEMBER — ALWAYS STORE YOUR CHARCOAL IN A DRY PLACE.

Wood

One can now purchase bags of vine wood cuttings, which produce a high heat for a very short time. The cuttings are easy to light and unlike charcoal (which is odourless when fully alight) they emit a faint aroma. Because they produce heat for a relatively short time, vine cuttings are suitable only for fast-cooking food, such as fish and small chicken pieces. The only realistic alternative to charcoal, and without doubt the oldest barbecue fuel, is to use hardwoods such as beech, oak, birch, ash, apple and cherry. One would perhaps normally use hardwood only when time is not a pressing factor and/or when charcoal is unavailable.

Pit barbecues (p. 21) require large quantities of hardwood and beach barbecues relatively modest quantities. Those lucky enough to own a house with a large open fireplace can burn down a quantity of hardwood and use the hot embers to spit-roast or grill over. (The appropriate ironmongery can be purchased at most good barbecue stockists.) Use dry hardwood no more than 3–4 inches (7·5–10 cm) in diameter; a stack large enough to leave sufficient embers to cook over will probably take about an hour to reach the 'ready' state. Try to keep the wood pieces in the main body of your wood-pile as uniform in size as possible so that the fire comes to a state of readiness in a fairly even fashion.

Gas

See p. 23.

Electricity

See p. 25.

Firelighters

WARNING: NEVER use petrol, lighter fluid, kerosene, naphtha, methylated spirits or similar volatile liquids to light your charcoal – IT IS DANGEROUS TO DO SO!

NEVER ADD MORE STARTER FLUID OF ANY KIND TO CHARCOAL WHICH HAS ALREADY BEEN IGNITED and appears not to be burning (the charcoal is quite likely to be glowing hot inside even if there are no visible signs of this on the charcoal's surface). SHOULD YOU WISH TO REKINDLE THE FIRE USE A SOLID FIRELIGHTER — IF IN ANY DOUBT IT IS SAFER TO START AGAIN FROM SCRATCH.

Lumpwood charcoal is, generally speaking, fairly easy to ignite but charcoal in the form of briquettes – especially if the char content is low – can prove to be more difficult. However, one should not experience any problems if the few basic rules of firemanship described on p. 41 are followed, using your preferred igniting agent.

Solid Firelighters

The traditional solid white block firelighter, available from ironmongers (now known as hardware stores) is an efficient, safe and cheap domestic fire starter. Made basically from urea formaldehyde and petroleum distillate, the firelighter comes in a block which can be easily broken up into smaller sections as required. When it has been lit the firelighter emits a rather unpleasant petroleum odour combined with a certain amount of black smoke for 10 minutes or so. Both the smoke and odour will have dissipated long before the fire is hot enough to cook over. When the sealed cellophane wrapper is torn open the blocks begin to lose some of their potency and in so doing slightly taint the air where they are stored.

These drawbacks have to a large extent been overcome by a new solid firelighter that is claimed to be both odourless and smokeless when burning. The cubes are packed individually, so the problem of deterioration does not occur.

Liquid Firelighters

Commercial liquid firelighters, substantially the same as paint thinners, are usually available in 0.75l and 1l plastic bottles. Performance is much the same, regardless of brand, but some have a safer flashpoint. Commercial liquid firelighters, unlike methylated spirits, petrol, kerosene and so on, are not volatile, but even so you should not liven up a charcoal fire by squirting more liquid on it.

Jellied Alcohol

Use of jellied alcohol, which is supplied in tubes like toothpaste, is fairly limited because of its high cost. It is, however, probably the most convenient ignition agent to take on barbecue picnics.

Jellied alcohol burns cleanly with a colourless flame that is rather difficult to discern in broad daylight, so if the wind snuffs out the flame this may not be noticed for some time.

Gas Torch

Fast results can be achieved by using one of the compact gas torches of the type commonly used by the home handyman for stripping paint. One can now also buy a specially designed lance which is screwed on to a disposable cylinder of butane gas. After lighting the tip it is inserted into the pile of charcoal.

Electric Fire Starters

Similar in shape to a tennis racquet minus the strings, the electric fire starter comprises an electric element connected to a handle. The cable connecting the starter to the mains is long enough to reach a barbecue sited outside the house. Portable electric fire starters provide a fast and clean method of getting the charcoal going and although somewhat expensive they are very economical in use.

Chimney

Starting a charcoal fire by using paper and kindling wood tends to be rather messy, and not particularly efficient, when compared to most of the methods already described. The process is made easier by using a chimney. Specially designed charcoal chimneys are fairly common in North America and on the Continent but not many have yet found their way on to the British market. It is not difficult to construct your own charcoal chimney using a tall tin. (Your local burger restaurant will probably let you have an empty giant frankfurter can.) The tin should be opened at both ends, the sharp edges turned over and air holes punched round the bottom end. Place the chimney on the barbecue fire-bowl or grate and stuff the bottom end with newspaper and kindling wood. Fill the chimney up with charcoal and then light the paper. When the charcoal has ignited remove the chimney, using a pair of tongs.

Self-igniting Charcoal

See p. 38.

Firemanship

A successful barbecue begins with a properly laid fire so a little time taken in its preparation will result in controlled, clean, carefree and economic cooking.

Preparing the Fire-bed

Some barbecues are fitted with a steel grill or cast-iron grate on which to lay the charcoal. Apart from ensuring that the grid, or grate, remains unclogged, no further preparation of the fire-bed is required; the air will circulate freely through the grate as the air above the fire is heated and rises.

Many small picnic barbecues and some brazier units do not incorporate a charcoal grate and many are not provided with air vents either. If you put charcoal directly on the bottom of the fire-bowl, the fire will start and spread very slowly. This can be partly overcome by laying down a base for the fire, either gravel or a commercial fire-base.

First line the fire-bowl of the barbecue (having removed the food grill and the pivot lift-pin if there is one) with heavy-duty aluminium foil. Use enough foil to cover the entire bowl and keep the foil lining in position by tucking the edge securely over the bowl's rim. If you use the foil shiny side up, this helps marginally to reflect the heat back towards the food grill. Apart from reflecting the heat, the lining protects the bowl's paintwork and makes subsequent cleaning or replacement of the fire-bed easier.

The next step is to pour in sufficient fire-base to cover the base of the bowl evenly to a depth of approximately 1½ inches (4 cm). If you are using gravel, it should be dry, clean river gravel approximately ¼ inch (6 mm) in diameter. The gravel should be washed clean after every four to six barbecues, in a bucket of hot soapy water. After rinsing it well, the gravel should be

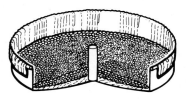

7   Section through a brazier barbecue showing how the fire-bowl is protected by aluminium foil and how the fire-bed is laid

thoroughly dried before using it again. Commercial fire-base, available from most barbecue stockists, is actually vermiculite; after the barbecue has been used several times it can be dumped in the garden (apparently it enriches the soil).

Preparing the Charcoal for Lighting

Different barbecues and differing cooking techniques require different approaches to preparing the fire, but it must always be borne in mind that charcoal – lump or briquette – will only take the fire from another lit piece if it is in actual contact with it, as there are no flames to leap across any gaps between the lit and unlit pieces.

For Cooking by Direct Heat (Grilling)

Prepare, if necessary, a fire-base (fig. 7) and build a pyramid-shaped pile of charcoal on it.

Using solid firelighter

Break off two or more pieces (depending on how impatient you are) and insert them among the charcoal about halfway up the pyramid. The starter will burn for approximately 15 minutes but the black smoke should have disappeared during the first 10 minutes or so. Make sure that all the pieces of solid starter have been completely burned away, for any that remain – the flame having been blown out perhaps by the wind – may re-ignite during cooking and taint the food. (If this does happen extract the offending piece quickly, using your long-handled tongs, and extinguish it.)

Using liquid firelighter

Follow the manufacturer's instructions carefully. These generally suggest that approximately 3–4 fl. oz (85–110 ml) should be squirted on to the cold fuel. Leave it to soak for a minute or so and then light the charcoal, using a long match or taper.

Care must be exercised if using liquid starter with a barbecue which has a separate charcoal grate and/or air vents in the fire-bowl, such as a kettle barbecue. Liquid applied to the charcoal may drain into and through the lower vents; it will lie outside the body of the barbecue and may be ignited accidentally later on (perhaps by a piece of hot coal dropping through the lower vent).

A small supply of briquettes can be kept soaking in the fluid (a wide-mouthed jar with an airtight screw-cap is ideal) to speed up the fire-starting process – just add three or four of the soaked briquettes or lumps of charcoal to the base of the pyramid, cover them up with untreated charcoal and light as above.

Using an electric fire starter

Simply place the element among the charcoal near the base of the pyramid and, after switching the power on, leave it for 5–10 minutes. Remove the element, remake the pile of charcoal and leave for a further 20–30 minutes, by which time the charcoal should be ready.

Using a gas torch

A gas torch is more effective if you arrange the charcoal one layer deep and crowded together. Pass the flame slowly over the charcoal until the fire has visibly started – grey patches glowing dully appear on the surface that the torch is playing on.

With a gas lance, light the tip, place it at the base of the pyramid and hold it there until the coals become ash-covered and start to glow.

Using jellied alcohol

Small amounts of the jelly should be squeezed from the tube on to the charcoal near the base of the pyramid. Close the tube and remove it before lighting the jelly.

For Spit-roasting

Prepare a fire-base if necessary. You can then either build a pyramid of charcoal and light it as described above, transferring the coals when ready (using a pair of long-handled tongs) to the back half of the fire-bowl (fig. 8), or

8   How to position the fire-bed and drip pan when spit-roasting

you can simply position the required quantity of charcoal directly in the back half of the fire-bowl and light it by the desired method.

A drip pan (see p. 61 for details of how to make a drip pan from aluminium foil) should be placed towards the front to catch the juices dripping off the meat as it swings forward and upwards.

For Cooking by Indirect Heat (in Covered Barbecues)

Virtually all covered barbecues incorporate charcoal grates so it should not be necessary to prepare a fire-bed.

Place an aluminium drip pan (an old roasting tin is ideal) in the centre of the grate and arrange an equal number of briquettes on each side of the pan. Place two or three pieces of solid firelighter in each pile or soak each pile with approximately 2 fl. oz (55 ml) of liquid firelighter. Ignite both piles of charcoal and leave until grey ash covers most of the surface area. It is important to keep an eye on how the fires progress as a strong wind may cause one pile of charcoal to burn faster while allowing the other pile to go out. It may be necessary at some point to transfer hot coals from one side of the pan to the other.

The Universal Barbecue

The Universal barbecue uses only one of its three bowls for fuel when spit-roasting or roasting, the remaining two being left empty to act as massive drip pans. The charcoal should be lit as described on p. 12.

The Amount of Fuel to Use

Novice barbecue chefs tend to use much more fuel than they actually require. Apart from being a waste, this can produce excessive heat and the meat will be heavily charred on the outside and somewhat raw inside. Practice will show how much charcoal is required; the following notes provide a rough guide. There are approximately sixty briquettes in an average 5 lb (2·3 kg) bag.

Hibachi, Picnic and Brazier Barbecues

Assuming you wish to use the complete area of the fire-bed, approximately forty-five briquettes will be required for a 24 inch (61 cm) diameter unit, allowing gaps of about 1 inch (2·5 cm) between the briquettes, and approximately twenty-five for an 18 inch (46 cm) diameter unit (smaller diameters pro rata). This amount of fuel should be enough to cook a full grill load of chicken pieces, steaks or chops, and the heat level should last for 1–1½ hours.

Kettle, Rectangular Covered, Wagon and Universal Barbecues

Sizes vary too much to be precise; generally speaking, these barbecues require less fuel than the open units detailed above.

Spit-roasting

Cooking, say, a 4 lb (1·8 kg) chicken or joint on a spit supported across a 24 inch (61 cm) fire-bowl will probably require twenty to twenty-four briquettes (fourteen to eighteen briquettes for an 18 inch, 46 cm fire-bowl). For larger pieces of meat add an extra layer of briquettes to give a cooking time of up to 2½ hours.

Controlling the Heat

When you have prepared the fire-bed and got the charcoal going well, you are left free to concentrate on controlling the heat and cooking the meat.

Heat control can be achieved by a variety of methods:

(a) by means of air vents (dampers) that form part of the covered barbecue design – the greater the draught, the fiercer the heat;

(b) by altering the distance between fire-bed and grill by means of levers, rotating grills, etc. (see p. 7);

(c) by increasing or decreasing the distance between individual briquettes once they are alight: the closer the briquettes, the more intense the resulting heat;

(d) since barbecue cooking is achieved not by flames but by the infra-red radiation given off by the coals, anything that inhibits this radiation slows the cooking process. It is therefore advisable to tap off excess ash on the charcoal periodically (perhaps by knocking the rim of the barbecue) – on the other hand the ashes may serve to dampen an over-hot fire.

For longer cooking sessions it is a good idea to keep a reserve of briquettes warming up around the edges of the active fire-bed. Cold briquettes when added to hot coals immediately diminish the general heat level, whereas a warmed-up briquette, when nudged up against a hot coal, will not have such an adverse effect.

Remember that every time the lid of a covered barbecue is raised during the cooking period – and perhaps kept in the raised position for a couple of minutes – the cooking time will have to be increased by another 5 minutes or so.

Flare-ups

Occasional flare-ups, usually caused by fat dropping directly on to hot coals, can be controlled with a fine water spray (see p. 30). When using an open barbecue it is possible to avoid flare-ups by arranging the fire-bed as shown (fig. 9); approximately one-third of the fire-bed is covered with briquettes set closely together (gaps of up to ½ inch, 12 mm), one-third by briquettes set about 2 inches (5 cm) apart and the remaining third either left empty or covered with a drip pan. The 'hot spot', where the briquettes are set very closely together, is used to seal the surfaces of the meat; the food can then be transferred to the area where the briquettes are further apart to continue cooking at a slower rate. The grill above the empty area of the fire-bed can be reserved for meat that is almost fully cooked (the heat from the adjacent areas will keep it warm). It is also useful as a parking place for meat that is exuding copious amounts of fat and could cause a major flare-up.

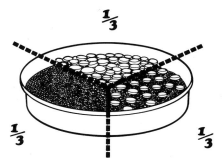

9   How to set up a fire-bed in a brazier barbecue to avoid flare-ups and achieve better cooking control

With practice, the chef should be able to use this arrangement of the grill to rustle up rare, medium and well-done steaks to order.

If the barbecue is tilted forward slightly, some of the fat will run down the grill bars away from the fire area; a narrow drip pan can be arranged to catch it (see p. 61).

Snuffing Out the Fire

Charcoal, when left to its own devices, will carry on burning until it is reduced to a fine ash, but this is wasteful if the cooking is finished and there is still plenty of charcoal left. In covered barbecues the fire can be snuffed out by closing the top and bottom dampers. The hot coals should be fully extinguished in 20 minutes or so. With smaller open units the hot coals can either be carefully transferred to a lidded coal bucket, which, when closed, will snuff out the fire, or they can be dunked into a pail of water and then left to dry out.

NEVER pour water over the barbecue itself to extinguish the coals – the sudden shock could well warp or damage the metal.

3 Cooking Techniques

Open Grill Cooking

Open grill cooking (grilling) is the most widely practised method of barbecue cooking. As the name implies, no cover or hood is used; covered barbecues can be used for grilling minus their lids.

Anything that can be cooked fairly quickly (half an hour or less) is a candidate for this method – steaks, chops, chicken pieces, hamburgers, sausages, whole small fish, fish steaks and skewered food.

General advice on grilling times is given in the table on p. 130; the speed of cooking is affected to a considerable degree by the strength of the wind and the ambient air temperature.

Tilting the barbecue forward slightly will help to avoid flare-ups; a narrow drip pan can be arranged to catch some of the fat (see p. 61).

Grilling Procedure

1. Start your fire, following the instructions in Part Two. Wait until most of the charcoal is covered with grey ash. Lightly knock some of the ash off before starting to cook.
2. Rub the grill bars with a little fat (perhaps cut from the steak or chop) or cooking oil to lubricate them. This will help prevent the meat from sticking to the grill during cooking.
3. If the barbecue design allows, adjust the food grill to a position 2–3 inches (5–8 cm) above the hot coals. Cooking at this level for a minute or so will sear the meat and help seal in the juices. After searing the meat raise the grill to 4–6 inches (10–15 cm) above the coals and complete the cooking process.

Notes

- Lean meats taste better when basted with a little oil or butter during cooking.
- Thick basting sauces containing sugar burn very easily so apply them only during the final few minutes that the meat is on the grill (or grill the meat over a lower heat).

Sweet and sour spare-ribs (on the plate) (p. 91), spiced orange glazed spare-ribs (p. 91).

- For a stronger flavour, and to help tenderize the meat, marinate it for a few hours prior to cooking (see p. 120).

Grilling on Skewers

For sheer versatility skewer-cooking takes some beating because it allows the chef free rein. Meat, poultry, fish, vegetables and fruit can all be cooked on skewers, separately or in mouth-watering combinations. The possibilities can be extended even further by marinating the meat and vegetables before cooking with wine, herbs and spices (see p. 120).

Metal skewers come in a variety of sizes. Those with flat blades are easier to turn; with round skewers the food may stay in the same position when the skewer is rotated. Saté is traditionally skewered on strips of bamboo (which should be soaked in water before use to prevent them from burning); these can usually be obtained from shops selling oriental food. (For further information on skewers see p. 29.)

Oiling the skewers before threading on the food will help to prevent the meat from sticking.

When skewering chunks of fish, leave the skin intact as this will help to hold the flesh together when the fish is cooking.

Selecting the contents of a skewer so that they are all cooked at the same time can be a problem, especially when mixing meat and vegetables. It might therefore be worth considering making up skewers with like food. Alternatively some foods, particularly chunks of pork, can be part-cooked before putting them on skewers with their faster-cooking items.

It is difficult to avoid a certain amount of flare-up when cooking kebabs on a small hibachi or picnic barbecue; if you have a larger barbecue you can arrange the hot coals in parallel rows 2–3 inches (5–8 cm) apart and position the skewers above the gaps between the rows. This should result in fewer flare-ups and better cooking control.

Spit-roasting

In many great houses during the Tudor/Elizabethan period dozens of chickens would be turned simultaneously on a multiple-spit-roaster like the one which can be seen at Hampton Court Palace. For some, the fascination of watching a chicken slowly turning on a spit is only matched by that of watching a man in a crane using a steel ball to demolish a building. Small wonder that cafés use a spit-roaster turning in the window to draw in the customers. It's not surprising therefore that an increasing number of barbe-

Barbecued crown roast (p. 81).

cues incorporate rotisserie equipment in their design and that DIY rotisserie attachments are sold in increasing quantities.

Details of the equipment are given on p. 29 and a time-chart on p. 129.

When spit-roasting or indirect cooking, particularly fatty meats, three-quarters fill the pan with water (left-over beer or wine will do just as well and add a bit of culinary mystique into the bargain). The temperature of the fat collecting in the drip pan will then be kept below the level where it could possibly ignite and cause a flare-up.

NEVER POUR WATER INTO A DRIP PAN THAT CONTAINS HOT FAT.

The Spit Balance Test

Having prepared the fire-bed for spit-roasting (p. 43) one then has to balance the food carefully on the spit. It is important that the spit should turn as evenly as possible – food rotating in fits and starts will result in uneven cooking and heavy wear on the motor. With practice, you should be able to pass the spit through the centre of the food regardless of its shape. In the case of rib roasts and other bone-in joints the spit should be run through the joint diagonally to make it balance. Push the spit into one of the cut sides near the point where the ribs begin to protrude and run it through towards the top of the other side. Before fully tightening the tines (spit-forks) a balance test should be carried out by holding the spit, as shown (fig. 10), to check its tendency to roll. Rotate the spit slowly on your palms – if there is no tendency to roll suddenly from any position, the balance is good. If it does roll unevenly, re-skewer the food to correct the imbalance. The use of balancing weights will certainly help, especially if one is spit-roasting very fat meat which constantly shifts its centre of gravity during cooking. When the food is balanced to the best of one's ability, the spit-forks should be fully tightened, with pliers if available. Some barbecues have a very restricted amount of space between the spit and fire-bed so it is important to truss chickens and other small birds firmly so that the wings and legs stay close to the body.

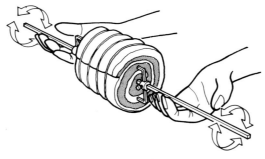

10   The spit balance test

11　How to impale a complete section of spare-ribs for spit-roasting

As well as chicken and leg of lamb try spit-roasting a complete rack of spare-ribs, pushing the spit through the tissue between the ribs so that you end up with an undulating, concertina-like formation (fig. 11). Large whole fish, after spitting, can be wrapped securely in a piece of chicken wire that has had the galvanizing burnt off (fig. 12), or well wrapped round with string.

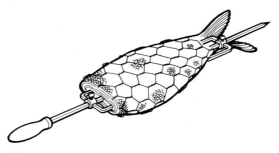

12　Wrapping a large fish in clean chicken wire (having burnt off the galvanized coating) will help to keep it intact and easier to handle when cooking it on a spit or by direct grilling

Another meat which is delicious when cooked on a spit is a complete calf's liver. The liver should be tied into a compact bundle before placing it on the spit; if you can get a caul (the fatty lace-like membrane that surrounds a pig's stomach) from your butcher this will act as an effective baster to keep the liver moist.

Indirect Heat Cooking

A covered barbecue can be used to cook by indirect heat – the equivalent of roasting or baking in a domestic oven. A glance at the cooking time-chart on p. 132 will show you that the owners of a covered unit can be truly ambitious when deciding what to tackle. With some experience behind them, many people use their barbecue to cook complete three- or four-course meals.

13   Where to place the drip pan in a covered barbecue when cooking by the indirect method

Whole birds, large joints, thick pieces of meat, bread, pies, cakes, pizzas, casseroles can all be cooked in the covered barbecue. Having set up the fire-bed and drip pan as described on p. 44 the joint is placed on the food grill in a position directly over the drip pan (or in the case of the Universal barbecue over one of the empty foil-lined fire-bowls). The heat from the charcoal or gas-heated volcanic rock reflects off all the inside areas of the barbecue, with the result that the food cooks evenly and is very succulent. In effect, the barbecue is acting very much like an oven and once the lid has been placed in position, very little attention – apart from some basting or the occasional addition of some more charcoal – is required until the joint has finished cooking.

When roasting fatty joints, using a drip pan part-filled with water will reduce the risk of a flare-up (see p. 50).

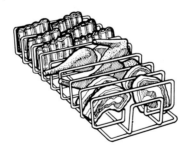

14   Using a rib rack in a covered barbecue will greatly increase the barbecue's capacity when cooking spare-ribs (sectioned or whole), chops, chicken quarters, and so on

Smoke-cooking

Smoke-cooking should not be confused with smoke-curing. Before the advent of food-freezing technology, meat and fish were preserved by smoke-curing, a cold smoking process, where temperatures were kept as low as 50°F (10°C); it could take several days or even weeks to complete. Smoke-cooking on the other hand is a 'hot' smoking process that is used to give the food extra flavour and a richer colour.

The prerequisite for smoke-cooking is a covered barbecue with a tight-fitting lid. Those who intend to do a lot of smoke-cooking can now buy purpose-made, portable smokers. These are made from sheet metal and are of a cylindrical shape with a close-fitting domed lid. They come complete with a grill to support the charcoal and aromatic smoking woods, a pan to hold water (or other liquid) and one or two grills to support the food to be smoked. Other purpose-made smokers (not at present available on the UK market) include the Chinese smoke oven and the Japanese earthenware smoker, known as a *kamado*.

Temperatures in the purpose-made portable smokers with their water pans sited between the coals and food, can be maintained at a slightly lower level (around 200°F, 95°C) than in a covered barbecue, where the ambient temperature would perhaps be closer to 275°F (135°C).

Having smoked your joints of meat (allowing approximately 1 hour per pound (450 g), you then finish cooking them on the barbecue (using the grill or the spit) or in the kitchen oven. The smoked food can be kept in the refrigerator for up to three days or deep frozen if you do not want to cook it immediately.

The smoke is produced from small logs, wood chunks or small chips of hardwoods (such as apple, hickory, cherry, oak and beech) placed on a small bed of charcoal that has reached the stage where it is completely covered in grey ash. The wood should have been soaked in water for at least an hour before putting it on the hot coals. During burning, the wood will give off a pleasant fragrance and this can be enhanced, or partially masked, if it becomes too pungent, by adding some sprigs of rosemary or thyme, or a few bay leaves.

Smoke-cooking in this way is a lengthy two-part affair. The alternative is to cook the meat fully for the usual time (which in a covered barbecue can be considerably shorter than normal oven times) while applying aromatic woods and herbs to the hot coals. The result will be a marked change in the colour of the meat (hickory, for example, can turn a chicken or turkey to a dark mahogany colour, depending on how much wood is used). The effect on the flavour tends, however, to be only skin deep when compared to food smoke-cooked by the slower, two-stage, method.

It is now possible to buy a range of barbecue burning woods and herb mixtures in small packs.

Spare-ribs, ham, poultry, trout, mackerel, eel, salmon, oysters, lamb, venison, pork, liver, sausages and kidneys are excellent foods for smoke-cooking and even processed cheese can be smoked if the barbecue or smoker can be controlled to give a very low heat. Baked beans placed in an open pot on the covered grill will take on a pleasant smoky flavour, but the exposed surface becomes a little crusty.

Plank Barbecuing

This technique, copied from the Red Indians by the American frontiersmen, requires an open fire – a camp bonfire or the home hearth. The materials required are very straightforward. You will need a solid hardwood plank at least 1 inch (2·5 cm) thick and just wide enough to give a 2–3 inch (5–8 cm) margin around the food. An old chopping board approximately 12 × 18 inches (30 × 46 cm) would do, as it will provide enough space for several steaks, but do not use pine or redwood planks. You will also need a length of stainless steel wire (about 10 ft, 3 m, should suffice for a board of the size suggested), a dozen 1½ inch (4 cm) round steel nails, a sheet of extra-thick aluminium foil, 6 house bricks, a bowl of water and a brush.

To prepare the board for cooking, knock the nails into the board, about 1 inch (2·5 cm) from the edge, in two equally spaced rows of six. The rows of nails should be opposite one another but staggered so as to give a zig-zag pattern when the wire is strung across the board. Leave the nails protruding about an inch (2·5 cm). Fashion the foil into a drip pan (see p. 61) long enough to sit the edge of the board in. The pan should be about 6 inches (15 cm) wide and about 1 inch (2·5 cm) deep.

Most flat foods normally barbecued by the direct grilling method can be plank-cooked, but the technique lends itself particularly well to oily fish such as herring and mackerel. The fish will cook better if filleted and laced to the board in butterfly fashion. The skins should be left on to help keep the flesh in place.

The fish should be brushed over with melted butter prior to cooking. Because of the distance of the board's surface from the heat of the open fire the cooking times are extended. As a rule of thumb one should allow twice the time it would take the same food to cook when being direct grilled some 6 inches (15 cm) above the fire-bed. Mackerel opened out as mentioned above would therefore take about 15–20 minutes to cook.

Plank Cooking Porterhouse Steak

You will need a porterhouse or large T-bone steak 1½–2 inches (4–5 cm) thick, oil and salt and freshly ground pepper.

Well oil one side of the board. Slash the fat at the edge of the steak at 2–3 inch (5–8 cm) intervals. Brush the steak all over with oil and season it with pepper. Sear one side of the steak to a rich golden colour (a hinged steak broiler is ideal for this task) and using the stainless steel wire, lace the meat into position, seared side down, on the oiled board.

Stack the bricks in a line three high, about 12 inches (30 cm) from the base of the fire. Prop the board against the bricks at as upright an angle as possible. The heat of the fire, distance of board from fire and the air temperature will obviously affect the cooking times, but the steak should be medium to well done in about 30–35 minutes. If the board surface begins to char, brush it with water. When ready, unlace the steak (using gloves and/or a pair of pliers) and carve directly from the board.

Selecting and Buying Meat for the Barbecue

Having taken considerable pains to seek out a barbecue and fuel it follows that one should exercise equal care in selecting the meat. Buying good-quality meat can make economic sense because there will be very little wastage, but if the purse strings have to be drawn fairly tight, one can, with the use of a good marinade (or flavoured meat tenderizer) barbecue less tender and cheaper cuts such as flank, blade and chuck. Ask your butcher's advice. The following will give you some guidelines.

Beef

The flesh of good-quality beef should be bright red with a brownish tinge and be firm to the touch; it should be marbled with small streaks of white fat which helps to produce tenderness and flavour when the meat is cooked. Very lean meat is sometimes tough and rather flavourless. The colour of the outer covering of fat should be creamy, although at certain times of the year it can have a yellowish appearance.

Avoid buying beef that has a very dark colour and looks somewhat dry, as this indicates the meat has, in all probability, come from an old animal or, alternatively, has been exposed to the air for too long.

There are numerous ways of cutting a carcass, but the names of the cuts given below are those most commonly used. Your butcher will be able to advise you of any local variations.

Fillet Steak

The fillet is taken from the undercut of sirloin and is a very expensive but very tender cut. Large pieces of fillet – they should weigh at least 2½ lb (1·1 kg) –

can be roasted and are easy to carve. Individual portions of 6–8 oz (170–225 g) should be grilled.

Sirloin

With the bone in, a sirloin joint should weigh not less than 3½–4 lb (1·6–1·8 kg) and should contain the undercut or fillet. Sirloin can be boned and rolled, but it has more flavour, and the meat is juicier, when roasted on the bone.

T-bone

Easily recognized by the shape of its bone, the T-bone steak is tender and has an excellent flavour. Ideally the steak should be 1½–2 inches (4–5 cm) thick and weigh approximately 1½ lb (0·7 kg). T-bone steak 1 inch (2·5 cm) thick weighs about ¾ lb (340 g).

Rib Steaks and Roasts

Top rib, fore rib and back rib are all similar cuts – the chief difference between them being the length of the rib bones. Fore rib, with the longest bones, can be made into a separate joint by cutting off the rib ends. Ribs can be grilled as they are or boned and rolled for spit cooking. A 1 inch (2·5 cm) thick rib steak weighs about 1 lb (450 g). The generous marbling of fat in these steaks gives them a very good flavour.

Flank

Flank varies in thickness according to which part of the animal's belly the cut is taken from. Thick flank is suitable for slow roasting and can be rolled for spit cooking. Flank has a strong flavour and is quite lean with rather coarse fibres.

Porterhouse

A tender and excellently flavoured steak, the porterhouse is a 1½–2 inch (4–5 cm) slice taken from the wing rib. A 1½ inch (4 cm) steak will weigh about 2 lb (0·9 kg) and should serve three to four people; it is not as easy to carve as sirloin.

Rump

Rump steak is considered to have the best flavour of all the steak cuts, but to be tender it must be well hung. One indication of this is its colour; the lean should have a purplish tinge and the fat should be creamy white. A large piece of rump, weighing 4–6 lb (1·8–2·7 kg), can be rolled, tied and spit-roasted, and will serve twelve to eighteen people. A 1 inch (2·5 cm) thick slice will weigh about 1½ lb (0·7 kg) and serve three to four people.

Chuck

Of fairly good flavour, chuck is a lean cut with very little, if any, fat. Unless the chuck steak is marinated and/or treated with a meat tenderizer, it will require long, slow cooking.

Lamb

Lean, good-quality lamb will vary from a light pink, for a very young lamb, to a fairly dark red for a mature sheep. A layer of fat should cover the legs and shoulders, and both of these joints should have a plump look about them. The colour of the fat will vary according to the origin of the animal. Home-produced lamb – only available from the butcher during the spring and early summer – will have creamy white fat and the fat of imported lamb will be white. Avoid buying lamb whose fat is yellowish and rather brittle as this will indicate either an old animal or one that has spent too long in the freezer.

Shoulder

Not a particularly good joint for barbecuing because the large proportion of bone to meat makes it rather extravagant. If you do want to barbecue shoulder, it should be boned and rolled or cut into small, boneless pieces for grilling or using for kebabs.

Leg

Unlike shoulder, leg of lamb has a large proportion of meat to bone. The best part of the leg for barbecuing is the fillet (top end). The leg can be roasted whole on the spit or, by the indirect heat method, in a covered barbecue. Alternatively the leg can be boned, the halves opened up ('butterflied') and cooked by either the direct or indirect method.

Chops

Ideally the chops bought for barbecuing should be about 1½ inches (4 cm) thick, with the minimum of bone. Loin or chump chops are therefore better than rib chops, and are particularly suitable for grilling. Another good cut is a steak or 'chop' from the leg.

Pork

The flesh of a young animal should be fine textured and pink. The meat of older animals is coarser and of a darker colour. The skin should feel smooth and firm to the touch and the meat of a young pig will contain very little gristle. Cut flesh should be slightly moist and contain small flecks of fat. The bones of a young animal should be small and pinkish in colour. Bones of older animals are an off-white colour.

Leg

The hind leg of the pig, weighing 10–12 lb (4·5–5·4 kg), can be barbecued whole or cut up into steaks or chops. When wet-cured in a brine solution, the hind leg, or sometimes the fore leg, becomes gammon, and may be smoked or unsmoked (green). Unsmoked gammon is milder in flavour than smoked.

Ham

This comes from the hind leg and is dry-cured (much more slowly than gammon) in a mixture of saltpetre and salt. Some experts do not recommend roasting smoked cured ham over charcoal but there is no harm in doing so if you stick to recommended cooking times and temperatures. Tinned cooked ham can be barbecued and will only require a few minutes' grilling to warm through and become lightly browned.

Loin

The loin is the best and most expensive joint. The whole loin, weighing 12–14 lb (5·4–6·4 kg), is usually cut into chops or several roasts. The choice centre cut, weighing about 4–5 lb (1·8–2·3 kg), can be boned, rolled and tied for cooking on the spit or cooked whole by the indirect cooking method.

Spare-rib

Spare-rib is probably the best-known and most popular cut of pork for barbecuing. The joint, which is fairly lean, comes from the area immediately behind the head and has a broad cut area where the blade, fore leg and hand have been sliced away. Allow about ¾ lb (340 g) per serving.

Chops

The most tender, best-flavoured and expensive chops come from the loin. Neck and chump chops are also suitable for grilling.

Hand and Spring (Fore Leg)

An awkwardly shaped joint which can be boned, rolled and tied for spit cooking, or boned and cut into small pieces for grilling or using for kebabs.

Sucking Pig

Most butchers and provision merchants will require at least a week's notice that you want sucking pig, as they will invariably have to obtain the pig from a large city meat market via their local wholesaler. High pig meat prices will also increase the difficulty of buying a sucking pig, simply because the producer will make more money from letting the piglet grow to full weight. The ideal weight is 15–20 lb (6·8–9·1 kg). A young pig, lighter in weight, would give very little more than skin and bones. Allow about 1 lb (450 g) per serving.

Veal

The least satisfactory meat for barbecuing, as it is very lean and has a tendency to become dry when cooked over a charcoal fire; its delicate flavour can be somewhat overpowered by the charcoal smoke.

Veal from milk-fed calves is very tender and considered superior to grass-fed veal although the latter has more flavour. The flesh of good-quality veal should be a very pale pink or off-white from milk-fed calves and a pale pink from grass-fed calves. The flesh should have a fine texture and be moist and soft – but not too flabby or wet. Flesh that has either a dry, pale brown or bluish appearance will be stale. Veal bones are pinkish white and very soft in comparison to those of mature animals. There is very little external fat and its colour will vary from pinkish white to a pale yellow tinge. The fat around the kidneys should be firm and very white.

An important point to consider, before buying veal for a barbecue, is that it keeps very badly and should be used within a few days of slaughter. It would therefore be wise to check with your butcher that he will have veal available when you need it.

Leg

The leg can be cooked complete with the bone or boned and rolled.

Shoulder

Although the shoulder can be roasted on the bone, its awkward shape usually results in its being boned, rolled and stuffed.

Chops

Usually cut from the loin. Chump chops have a round bone in their centre and are cut from the bottom end of the loin. They can be grilled.

Estimating the Cooking Temperature

It's worth repeating that one should never start cooking on a barbecue until the fire-bed has reached the correct level of heat. Without the aid of an air-thermometer (sometimes included with covered barbecues) there are two basic methods one can follow:

1. Visually assessing the state of readiness the coals have reached. One can safely proceed if at least 80 per cent of the surface area of the briquettes or lumps of charcoal are covered with a grey ash.
2. Roughly estimating the temperature 1 inch (2·5 cm) or so above the level of the food grill. This can be done by placing the hand, palm side down, just above the grill and judging the temperature by the number of seconds the hand can be kept in position before the heat becomes too intense. The weakness of this method is the variation in the sensitivity of the palm of the hand from one chef to another, but even the horniest-handed chef will be unwilling to remain above fierce heat for a second longer than a person with soft skin! The seconds can be counted off in the following manner (to oneself, of course): 'a thousand and one', 'a thousand and two' and so on. If you are forced to withdraw your hand at or before the count of 'one thousand and two', the charcoal can be classified as hot. However, if you can count up to 'a thousand and four', the fire can be classified as only medium hot. Most food cooked will require cooking at the higher heat level.

    To estimate the temperature when preparing to spit-cook hold the hand cautiously, palm side down, 3–4 inches (7·5–10 cm) below the level of the spit. Heat calculations are then carried out as above.

4 Tricks of the Trade

Making a Drip Pan from Aluminium Foil

The use of a drip pan is part and parcel of virtually all the barbecuing techniques described on the previous pages. Making your own drip pan is a very simple matter.

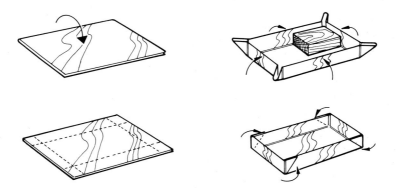

15   How to make a drip pan out of aluminium foil

Take an 18 inch (46 cm) roll of extra-thick (heavy-duty) aluminium foil and tear off a strip about 3 inches (7·5 cm) longer than the length of the pan you need. Fold the foil in half lengthwise, shiny side out. Use a piece of wood, or the side of a book, to help form the side and end walls of the pan which should be about 1–1½ inches (2·5–4 cm) high. Alternatively, simply score all the way round about 1–1½ inches (2·5–4 cm) in from the edge. Pull out the corners as shown in the sketch, and fold back tightly against the sides. The result should be a leak-proof tray approximately 6 inches (15 cm) wide with sides 1–1½ inches (2·5–4 cm) high.

Using wider foil will allow you to increase the thickness and strength of the pan.

Making a Cover for an Open Barbecue from Foil and Wire

For those who own an open brazier or small round picnic barbecue and would like to try their hand at cooking by the indirect method – possibly before buying a covered barbecue – here is an easy and economical way to make a temporary cover:

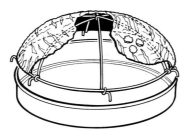

16   An improvised hood on a brazier barbecue allows it to be used for smoke-cooking or indirect heat cooking of meat or fish

1.   Make a ring corresponding exactly to the diameter and circumference of your barbecue's fire-bowl from 22-gauge galvanized steel wire. Lash the ends of the wire where they lap together with thin wire.
2.   Bend three equal half hoops from the thick wire and lash them together where they cross at the top, and where they cross the ring at right angles. The half hoops should extend past the ring by about 1 inch (2·5 cm) and the short pieces of extended wire should be shaped with a pair of pliers to allow the hood to sit snugly on the rim of the fire-bowl. The resulting frame should resemble an upturned hanging flower basket.
3.   Cover the frame with strips of extra-thick aluminium foil, dull side out, ensuring that the seams are folded tightly together.
4.   Carefully puncture a couple of small holes, about the thickness of your finger, near the apex of the cover.

   For those who own a small picnic barbecue and a wok, using the wok upside down will do the trick.

Organizing Barbecue Parties

Large-scale Barbecue Parties

To some a large-scale barbecue party will mean entertaining twenty-five guests while to others 250 guests would represent a fairly modest exercise.

Whatever the numbers involved, and that includes a small family affair, each party demands a considerable degree of forward planning for it to be a success. The planning should include the one thing you cannot predict – the weather. With really large-scale parties this can be a big headache unless one is fortunate enough to have the use of a location that includes such buildings as open-sided barns.

Family parties, where the number of guests is perhaps in the order of thirty or forty, are less of a problem. Providing there is adequate back-up accommodation, your contingency plans should be concentrated on providing shelter for the chef(s) and barbecue equipment, as the guests will probably be just as happy sitting indoors as they would have been sitting in the garden. As long as the food is tasty and plentiful, the party will still go with a swing!

The nature and extent of the menu will be shaped mainly by the type, size and number of barbecues available and by your budget. You should have no great difficulty in borrowing or hiring the number of barbecues needed to cope with the food, and it is far better to end up with extra cooking capacity than to be short. Remember that most shops which hire out equipment such as cement mixers and floor polishers, also hire out charcoal- and gas-burning units. There is also an increasing number of garden centres which do likewise – but remember to book your barbecue in good time.

There is a lot to be said for concentrating on basically simple food, such as chops, burgers, sausages, chicken or turkey pieces, steaks, spare-ribs; in fact, you will have to do this if the barbecues you are using are of the open variety, e.g. the brazier type barbecue. However, with luck there will be at least one covered barbecue at your disposal and this will open up opportunities to cook something that is both economical and good to look at. You could, for example, smoke-cook a large turkey which, allowed to rest for about 20 minutes after cooking, will carve both beautifully and bountifully. Alternatively, with a covered barbecue you could cook a whole ham that has been prepared in the classic style with the fat scored criss-cross fashion, studded with whole cloves and basted with a brown sugar glaze. Although a fully cooked York ham weighing, say, 15 lb (6·8 kg) is an expensive item by itself, when properly carved it will cater for up to sixty people – considerably more if the menu includes a slice or two of turkey, plus a sausage. A fully cooked ham will require only about 10 minutes to the pound (455 g) to reach serving temperature.

Cooking some of the food on a covered barbecue, which can be left to look after itself to a large degree, will also help to cut down on the chef's workload, as will encouraging the guests to do some self-catering. Providing you can gather together sufficient skewers and basting brushes, most people will enjoy grilling kebabs over a charcoal fire. All you then have to do is to assemble bowls or trays of assorted food – cubes of lamb, pork, beef, ham, pieces of sausage, lamb kidneys, fresh mushrooms, squares of green peppers, small tomatoes, pineapple pieces – plus sufficient bowls of basting sauce. You should also have ready an adequate supply of good-quality paper napkins for the guests to protect their hands while turning the skewers.

Before letting your guests loose with their skewers and bowls of food, make sure that the fire-beds in the communal barbecues are in good heart, i.e. that the charcoal is completely covered in grey ash and will not require stoking up for at least 30–40 minutes. Also ensure that the food grills are not positioned too closely or too far from the fire – 4–6 inches (10–15 cm) above the coals is ideal.

In order to make kebabs go further you can have ready a quantity of pitta bread, cut in half either lengthways or crosswise, for the guests to stuff with their cooked kebabs and freshly prepared green salad.

Fresh air certainly stimulates one's appetite and eating al fresco can be relied upon to increase a normal food intake considerably. As a rough guide reckon on serving 6–8 oz (170–225 g) of boneless lean meat per adult guest. Apart from a small steak the lean meat content of the menu could be made up by slices of turkey or chicken meat, ham, pork, lamb or veal. The weight allowance should be increased to around 12–16 oz (340–440 g) per head if meat on the bone is being offered exclusively, e.g. spare-ribs or chops. Costs will be reduced quite considerably if, say, up to a half of the fare is made up of sausages or burgers. In fact, some guests would be quite upset if a glorious barbecued banger was not on offer.

In my experience, salads for barbecue parties tend to be available in excessive quantities – probably because volunteers who bring their own specially concocted salad tend to be somewhat over-zealous. It is, however, better to have too much of everything, particularly because appetites always seem to revive two or three hours after the meal has been consumed.

Apart from meat and salad the main part of the meal is usually supplemented by chunks of French bread, bread rolls or pitta bread (as mentioned above). Baked potatoes are always very popular but they keep the chef busy for at least an hour before beginning on the direct grilled meat. Once the potatoes have been baked, they must be kept hot. This requires either extra barbecue capacity or the construction of a hay box. In the latter, the potatoes are well wrapped around with foil, newspaper and/or wood shavings and thus are kept acceptably hot for about an hour.

An alternative to barbecue baked potatoes is to use the kitchen oven or, where large numbers are involved, to enlist the services of your friendly local baker. In fact, a baker can be a godsend for the organizers of large-scale barbecues. When your guests number hundreds rather than dozens, you will find yourself unable to feed everyone simultaneously. People at the end of the queue usually have to wait patiently while their food is cooked – sometimes virtually from scratch.

Assuming most large-scale barbecues take place on a Saturday evening, try to arrange for the baker to run the meat through after the last batch of bread has been baked on Saturday morning. Bakers' ovens probably vary a little in design but the one I am familiar with has large pans (each one accommodating several loaves of bread) which slowly circulate around the hot oven. Before placing the meat it may be necessary to cover the base of the pans with aluminium foil. Chicken and/or turkey pieces should be almost fully cooked so that in the evening they will need only a few minutes of grilling over hot coals, and basting with a tasty barbecue sauce, before serving.

Fund-raising Barbecues

Holding a barbecue to raise money for a club, association or charity is now fairly commonplace. However, you should remember that the cost of hiring a large marquee will inevitably swallow up a large slice of income. The first task, therefore, for the organizer(s) is to select a location that can 'absorb' people should it rain.

As we have already seen, catering for large numbers, i.e. more than fifty or sixty people, demands a high level of forward planning. It will also demand an adequate level of cooperation and support from others to ensure that everything goes smoothly. Although this is not a pro rata figure, one should be thinking in terms of ten people to cater for, say, 100–150 guests. This number is obviously related to the type of food being cooked and served and, to a lesser extent, to the number of barbecues being used. Assuming your selected site is a secure one with only one entrance you will require at least one person, preferably two, on the gate. If it is to be a late-evening/night-time barbecue one of the team must be responsible for obtaining and handling the necessary lighting equipment. Controlling sufficient barbecues to cater for 100–150 people will require two or three chefs, again depending on the type of food being cooked and how much of it has been pre-cooked.

To keep the queues for food as short as possible it is a good idea to have more than one serving point. A good lay-out, which should be able to cope fairly comfortably with up to 200 people, is to have four trestle tables butted end to end in a straight line. The two outer tables can be laid out with cutlery, plates and napkins, and perhaps bread rolls, and the two inner tables can be used to dispense the meats. A further table set at right angles behind one of the outer tables can be used for carving joints; thus making it relatively easy to keep the servers at the centre tables well supplied.

Ideally, each centre table should have two servers and the barbecues should be set in line some 10 ft (3 m) directly behind them in order to keep the food line flowing. Two queues of guests should approach the serving tables via the outer tables and then move smartly away to pick up salad, sauces, etc., laid out on one or more tables well away from the queues in order to avoid entanglement.

By siting the barbecues behind, or hemmed in by, the serving tables, you should avoid the problem of children, or tipsy adults, accidentally knocking into them. If children are present, do not leave the barbecues unattended after the food has been cooked as the charcoal remaining – unless immediately doused – will continue to burn and stay very hot for another two hours or so.

The drinks table or bar should also be sited well clear of the cooking/serving area. It is advisable to check with your local magistrate's court before committing yourself to selling alcohol or beer at the barbecue. Favoured hot-weather warm-evening drinks are beer, table wine, home-made lemonade, cider and cold punch. Mulled ale would be a good standby for a cooler evening. Because of the quantities involved, your local pub may be willing to take over the bar allowing you a modest profit in return for the work.

Bearing in mind that the helpers will probably be in need of a rest when sweet time comes around, it might be politic to offer something like fresh fruit, ice-cream, gâteau or fresh fruit salad and cream. However, if you want to include a barbecue sweet there are many choices in the recipe section of this book. Perhaps the simplest, but involving quite a bit of preparation, is Grilled Bananas République (see p. 117). If you plan to provide hot coffee, calculate on at least two cups per person.

In addition to the serving tables, as many other tables and chairs as possible should be set out for the guests to use. Generally speaking, the village hall or its equivalent will be happy to hire out furniture, but remember to make your booking well in advance.

Having talked earlier about varying the menu to include large joints (by using covered barbecues) it must be said that extra-large barbecues involving several hundred people must perforce concentrate on fast open grill cooking, i.e. steaks, chops, burgers, chicken pieces and sausages. In order to cope with the heavy demand one can make frames for large barbecues from commercial slotted steel angle and the grills from steel mesh or expanded metal. These barbecues can be as long as required, 20 ft (6 m) or more, but for controlled and comfortable cooking their width should be restricted to no more than 30 inches (76 cm).

Rubbish – large-scale barbecues beget large amounts of garbage. Ensure that there are numerous dustbins, tea-chests, large cardboard boxes, large plastic or paper refuse sacks scattered about; this will make cleaning up after the party that much easier.

Children's Barbecue Parties

Organizing a children's barbecue party is one thing, but organizing the children is another! Detailed planning is therefore even more important because young children in particular can become quickly bored, and bored children and barbecues simply do not mix. You will need a menu of games to occupy them before and after the eating section of the party.

Young children up to, say, the age of twelve will need to be fed and watered by their adult supervisors (of whom you cannot have too many) but older children love to barbecue a burger, banger or fruit kebab they have prepared themselves. For some reason children love baked beans so a pot of Christine's Barbecued Baked Beans (see p. 114) is bound to go down well.

The priorities, as far as food is concerned, should be simplicity and plentifulness. Tomato ketchup will probably be appreciated more than a carefully prepared barbecue sauce. Small jacket potatoes with a special filling are popular, as are barbecue buns. While the food is being cooked, have plenty of crisps on hand to keep hunger at bay without ruining appetites. You can't go far wrong with sweets such as ice-cream or barbecued foil-wrapped chocolate banana split (chips of dark chocolate and pieces of marshmallow nestling in a wedge cut out along the length of the banana).

The best drinks to offer (complete with the longest possible straws) are fruit squashes, or well-chilled bottled minerals. Finally, when sending out invitations to the 'DIY' children, include a reminder for them to bring an apron and oven gloves.

5 Barbecuing — The International Scene

The dividing line between cooking food outdoors for pleasure rather than necessity unfortunately remains inviolate in most Third World countries. This line is, however, constantly being breached in more and more places around the world. In her book *Picnic*, Claudia Roden writes that barbecuing, though not a traditional Chinese method of cooking, is becoming very popular in Hong Kong – no doubt due to the influence of Western culture.

Sunny climates and an affluent society seem to be the perfect 'recipe' for the quick spread of barbecuing once it has been introduced into a country. There are therefore probably no greater devotees of the art than the Australians. Although Australia's industry turns out some pretty sophisticated gas barbecues, the emphasis, according to the few enthusiasts I have spoken to, is on the straightforward grilling of massive good-quality steaks (washed down, no doubt, by copious cans of lager). As a northern European I particularly envy the custom of enjoying a barbecued lunch on Christmas Day!

For many years now I have been hearing about the wonderful South African *braais*. The *braai* (meaning 'barbecue' and pronounced 'brie') takes many forms, from a rudimentary fire-pit to a converted oil-drum, and many homes have built-in *braaivleis* (literally 'burnt meat') pits. Typical of the foods cooked on the *braai* are sosaties (a kind of kebab), but keen chefs pride themselves on their home-made *boerewors* (farmers' sausage), a highly spiced mixed beef and pork sausage. Served as an accompaniment is stiff patu porridge made with corn (mealie) meal.

A *hangi* is to a New Zealander what a *braai* is to a South African. Its construction is traditionally carried out whenever possible by a Maori. Formerly much ceremony and ritual accompanied the making of a *hangi* but nowadays it is simply the prelude to a party or celebration.

Like all forms of pit barbecue, the *hangi* varies in size and construction from locality to locality. However, a typical *hangi*, catering for thirty or so people, would require the digging of a circular hole in the ground about 6 inches (15 cm) deep and 3 ft (90 cm) in diameter. A similar hole is then dug some 2 ft (60 cm) away. Paper and sufficient brushwood or kindling are then placed in the first hole to fill it. Lengths of slow-burning dry hardwood (the Maori would try to use manuka wood), 3 inches (8 cm) or more in diameter and about 4 ft 6 inches (135 cm) long, are laid side by side to cover the hole. Another layer of wood is placed crosswise to the first, followed by three or four more layers in a similar fashion. Over the wood place enough stones to fill the pit – they should make a layer at least 1 ft (30 cm) thick. The stones, which should be dry and hard, should be positioned so that the whole layer is slightly raised in the centre.

The *hangi* is usually prepared the day before the feast and covered overnight to protect it from rain. The wood is set alight about four hours before the meal is to be served. After the wood has been burning for about two hours the stones are separated from the charred wood and placed in the second hole to cover its bottom and sides. A piece of wire netting or a large grating is then placed across the hot stones. Meat, preferably cut into meal-sized portions, and whole chickens are wrapped in aluminium foil and then placed on the netting. They are sprinkled over with about ½ gallon (approximately 2l) of water, then covered with a sheet of calico that has been previously soaked in water. The entire *hangi* is then covered with two or three layers of wet sacking and this in turn is covered with a 6 inch (15 cm) layer of soil – care being taken to cover any vents through which steam can escape. Potatoes may be cooked separately in pots or directly in the *hangi*. The *hangi* is then left alone for 2–2½ hours before being carefully uncovered. The food (*kai*) is then taken out and served hot. Speed is essential so something like six people are required to place and cover the food.

America is undoubtedly the land of the barbecue cook-out. Sales of barbecue units are estimated to be running at well over 5 million annually and there are now around 125 million barbecues in regular use. During the past thirty years or so the American barbecue market has changed quite considerably and every year sees a growth in sales of gas barbecues and a fall in sales of the basic charcoal burning models like the hibachi. In fact, just over the border in Canada the barbecue market is dominated by the gas burning versions to such an extent that the charcoal burning units have only a 20 per cent share of the market.

Most public parks and picnic places in North America feature permanent built-in barbecues and there are even some restaurants which specialize in DIY barbecue meals where the customers, having selected and bought their steaks, proceed to one of several barbecue units in the restaurant's grounds to cook the food exactly as they like it.

Barbecuing in America has certainly come a long way from the days when the first chuck-wagon set off from Texas on its three-month trail drive north, rustling up wholesome steak and beans for hungry cowhands.

6 The Recipes

Recipe Codes

  = Spit-roasting

   = Direct heat cooking

= Indirect heat cooking

APPETIZERS

Bacon-wrapped Appetizers

A half slice of streaky bacon makes a tasty and self-basting overcoat for a wide variety of appetizers. Most of the following can be cooked together on the same skewer but when catering for large numbers it is easier if you stick to just one or two different kinds. If, however, you intend asking your guests to help, two or three different ones can be impaled on a 6 inch (15 cm) skewer and kept in the refrigerator until needed. Alternatively, secure individual, wrapped appetizers with wooden cocktail sticks that have been soaked in water. Don't forget to have an adequate supply of basting brushes to hand.

a selection from: small button mushrooms; pineapple chunks; small pieces of
    frankfurter sausage; small pieces of pre-cooked sausage; raw scallops; pre-cooked
    prawns; water chestnuts; sautéd chicken livers
bacon for wrapping each appetizer
sauces for basting (see pp. 124–6)

Cook the appetizers on a grill, set about 4–6 inches (10–15 cm) above low-to-medium hot coals, until the food is hot and the bacon is crisp and browned. Baste with a sauce during cooking.

Chicken Wings Teriyaki

Makes 20

10 chicken wings
Teriyaki Marinade (p. 121)

Disjoint the wings and discard the bony tips. Marinate them for 2–3 hours or overnight in a refrigerator. Reserving the marinade, drain the wings and grill over medium hot coals for about 15 minutes or until a dark crusty brown. Baste frequently with the marinade during cooking.

    The wing pieces will be difficult to handle in quantity unless they are securely held in a large closely meshed hinged basket (see p. 32). Remember to oil the inside of the basket before putting the food into it.

Prawns With a Hint of Mint   *(Plate 2)*

Makes
approximately 60

2 lb (0·9 kg) raw prawns, medium-sized,
   shelled and de-veined

Marinade
1 clove garlic, crushed
1 tsp salt
¼ tsp ground black pepper

1 tsp chilli powder
1 tbsp wine vinegar
1 tsp dried basil
1 tbsp fresh mint, finely chopped, or
  1 tsp dried mint
¼ pt (140 ml) oil

Combine the marinade ingredients in a bowl and blend well. Add the prawns
and turn until well coated with the mixture. Cover and refrigerate for at least
5 hours.

   Reserving the marinade, drain the prawns. Thread on to skewers and cook
on a well-greased grill, set 4–6 inches (10–15 cm) above medium hot coals, for
about 6–8 minutes, turning once. Baste frequently with the marinade during
cooking.

Spicy Grilled Prawns   *(Plate 2)*

Makes
approximately 60
(serves 6–8 as an
entrée)

2 lb (0·9 kg) raw prawns, medium-sized,
   shelled and de-veined
3½ tbsp melted butter or margarine

Marinade
1 tsp salt
½ tsp ground black pepper
½ tsp garlic powder

4 tbsp chilli sauce
4 tbsp wine vinegar
2 tbsp Worcestershire sauce
4 tbsp parsley, finely chopped
3½ tbsp oil

Combine the marinade ingredients in a bowl and blend well. Add the prawns
and turn until well coated with the mixture. Cover and refrigerate for 1–3
hours.

   Reserving the marinade, drain the prawns. Thread on to skewers and cook
on a well-greased grill, set 4–6 inches (10–15 cm) above medium hot coals, for
about 6–8 minutes, turning once. Baste frequently with the marinade,
blended with the melted butter or margarine, during cooking.

Porky Titbits

Serves 6

1 lb (450 g) lean pork tenderloin, cut into
    bite-sized thin strips
1 small fresh pineapple, peeled and cut
    into bite-sized chunks
1 medium green pepper, cleaned and cut
    into ¾ inch (19 mm) squares

Marinade
3 tbsp soy sauce
2 tbsp oil
½ tsp sugar
⅛ tsp cinnamon
1 clove garlic, crushed
2 dashes hot red pepper sauce
pinch of ground cloves

Combine the marinade ingredients in a bowl and blend well. Add the meat
and turn until well coated with the mixture. Cover and refrigerate for about 2
hours, stirring two or three times.

Reserving the marinade, drain the meat. Thread the meat, pineapple and
green pepper on to heavy bamboo skewers. If following the indirect method,
arrange skewers on cooking grill over a drip pan; cover barbecue and cook for
about 15 minutes, or until meat is done, turning two or three times. If cooking
by the direct method, turn the skewers more frequently and allow 10–12
minutes. Baste frequently with the marinade during cooking.

Protect your hand with an oven glove before turning the kebabs.

Barbecued Beef Bites

Makes
approximately 40

2 lb (0·9 kg) sirloin of beef, cut into
    bite-sized pieces
2 inch (5 cm) piece of fresh ginger root,
    peeled and sliced
2 small onions, chopped
½ tsp minced garlic

4 oz (115 g) sugar
scant ½ pt (280 ml) soy sauce
8 small dried chilli peppers or 1 tsp chilli
    powder
2 tbsp red wine vinegar
4 tsp cornflour

Combine the ginger, onions, garlic, sugar, soy sauce, chilli peppers and wine
vinegar. Heat in small pan for about 20 minutes, or until slightly thick. Blend
cornflour with ¼ pt (140 ml) water. Gradually add to sauce and keep stirring
until the mixture is clear and has thickened. Pour the mixture through a wire
strainer, pressing out all the juices. Discard the pulp and allow the mixture to
cool. Add the beef pieces and allow to stand for approximately 2 hours. Thread
two or three pieces of meat on to each skewer and cook over medium coals,
turning often, for about 10 minutes or until the beef is cooked to the required
degree.

BEEF

T-bone with Rosemary   *(Plate 6)*

Serves 4–6

T-bone steak, 1½–2 inches (4–5 cm) thick
2 tbsp fresh or 2 tsp dried rosemary
salt and pepper

Press equal portions of the rosemary into both sides of the meat. Allow it to stand at room temperature for approximately 30 minutes.

Barbecue over medium coals using the indirect cooking method, turning once, for about 15 minutes each side for rare meat. Season with salt and pepper and cut the meat across the grain in thin slanting slices.

Barbecued Rib Roast

rib roast or wing rib
(with bone in, allow ¾ lb (340 g) per serving)
salt and pepper

Trim excess fat from the meat and rub salt and pepper into it. If the bone is taken out tie securely with twine at approximately 1 inch (2·5 cm) intervals. Insert a meat thermometer into the thickest part of the roast with the point away from the bone or a pocket of fat.

Cook over medium coals by either the indirect method (see p. 51) or by spit-roasting, to desired degree (see time-charts on p. 131–2). Allow to rest for about 15 minutes before carving.

Steak au Poivre Flambé

Serves 4

4 steaks, ¾ inch (2 cm) thick
2 tbsp black peppercorns
2 large tomatoes
2 oz (55 g) butter or margarine
oregano
pinch garlic salt
4 tbsp brandy

Crush the peppercorns coarsely with a rolling pin and press into both sides of the meat. Allow it to stand at room temperature for approximately 30 minutes to absorb the flavour.

Cook over hot coals to the required degree and transfer to a hot dish.

Thickly slice the tomatoes and sauté in melted butter in a frying pan until the slices are hot through. Season with oregano and garlic salt to taste. Arrange the tomato slices on top of the steak. Warm the brandy, ignite and spoon, flaming, over the meat.

Chuck Burgers

Serves 8

1 lb (450 g) finely minced chuck steak
1 green pepper, finely chopped
1 small onion, finely chopped
2 medium carrots, grated
2 sticks celery, finely chopped
2 tsp Worcestershire sauce
1 clove garlic, crushed

1½ tbsp oil
pinch salt
¼ tsp ground black pepper
1 egg
8 soft rolls
8 slices of tomato

Lightly mix together the minced steak, green pepper, onion, carrots, celery, Worcestershire sauce, garlic, oil, salt and pepper, and bind with the egg. Shape into 8 burgers and cook on the grill, over hot coals, for approximately 20 minutes turning once. Toast the rolls during the last few minutes of cooking. Place a tomato slice on each burger and serve in the rolls.

Cheese and Bacon Burgers

Serves 6

1½ lb (0·7 kg) finely minced chuck steak
¾ tsp salt
pinch ground black pepper (optional)
4 tbsp Cheddar cheese, grated
3 rashers bacon (streaky or back)
6 soft rolls

Lightly mix together the minced steak, salt and pepper. Shape into 6 burgers and cook over hot coals for approximately 20 minutes, turning once. Shortly after turning, sprinkle the grated cheese on the patties and start grilling the bacon rashers. When crisp, the rashers should be diced and scattered over the melting cheese. Toast the rolls during the last few minutes of cooking and serve with the burgers.

Woganburgers

Serves 8

2 lb (0·9 kg) finely minced beef
1½ oz (45 g) soft white breadcrumbs
2 medium potatoes, peeled and grated
2 eggs
1 tsp salt
freshly ground pepper
4 slices processed cheese
garlic salt (optional)
8 soft rolls

Lightly but thoroughly mix together the minced beef, breadcrumbs, grated potatoes, 2 lightly beaten eggs, salt and pepper. Shape into 16 thin burgers. On 8 burgers place half a slice of processed cheese and sprinkle with a little garlic salt if desired. Top with the remaining burgers and press edges firmly together to seal.

Cook on the grill over hot coals for approximately 20 minutes turning once, or until nicely browned. Toast the rolls during the last few minutes of cooking and serve with the burgers.

Soy Chilli Burgers

Serves 4

1 lb (450 g) finely minced chuck steak
1 small onion, finely chopped
¼ tsp dry mustard
2 tsp soy sauce
1½ tbsp chilli sauce
2 tsp horseradish sauce
4 soft rolls

Lightly mix together all the ingredients (except the rolls) and shape into 4 burgers.

Cook on the grill over hot coals for approximately 20 minutes turning once, or until nicely browned. Toast the rolls during the last few minutes of cooking and serve with the burgers.

Burgers with Piquant Sauce

Serves 8

2¼ lb (1 kg) lean minced beef
1 tsp salt
½ tsp ground black pepper
1 medium onion, finely chopped

Sauce
2 tbsp Worcestershire sauce
4 tbsp tomato ketchup
½ tsp prepared English mustard
1 tbsp clear honey
2 tsp lemon juice

Thoroughly mix together the beef, salt and pepper and onion. Shape into 8 burgers.

Combine all the sauce ingredients in a pan with 2 tbsp of water and heat, stirring well.

Place the burgers on a greased grill about 5 inches (13 cm) above medium coals, and brush generously with the sauce. Cook for about 4 minutes each side if preferred rare, and 6–8 minutes for medium. Heat the remaining sauce and serve with the burgers.

Ginger Teriyaki

Serves 6

2 lb (0·9 kg) sirloin steak, cut into ¼ inch (6 mm) thick slices

Marinade
4 fl. oz (110ml) soy sauce
1 tbsp ground ginger
2 fl. oz (60ml) saké or sherry
1 clove garlic, minced
1–3 tsp sugar (according to taste)

Combine the marinade ingredients in a bowl and blend well. Add the meat and turn until well coated with the mixture. Marinate for approximately 1 hour.

Reserving the marinade, drain the meat. Thread it on to skewers, using one skewer for each strip of meat. Cook over hot coals for 1–2 minutes only each side, basting with the marinade.

Tangy Steak Strips

Serves 8

1 lb (450 g) boneless sirloin steak

Marinade
8 tbsp soy sauce
2 oz (55 g) brown sugar
4 tbsp dry sherry
1 tbsp oil
1 tsp ground ginger
1 small clove garlic, minced

Partially freeze the steak and cut into strips 6 inches (15 cm) long by 1 inch (2·5 cm) wide by ⅛ inch (3 mm) thick. Place in shallow pan.

Combine the marinade ingredients and mix well. Pour over steak strips and marinate for about 30 minutes. Drain and thread the strips of meat on to 6–8 inch (15–20 cm) bamboo skewers (metal skewers will do).

Cook to individual taste over medium coals, turning frequently. Serve hot with your favourite barbecue sauce.

Spit-roasted glazed shoulder of lamb (p. 82).

LAMB

Spit-roasted Stuffed Leg of Lamb

Serves 8

1 boned leg of lamb (approx 6 lb/2·7 kg)
2 oz (50 g) melted butter

Stuffing
1 green pepper, finely chopped
3 medium onions, finely chopped

3 cloves garlic, minced
2 small dried chilli peppers
½ tsp salt
¼ tsp ground black pepper
2 tsp ground cumin

Combine the stuffing ingredients and pound into a paste in a mortar. Spread the mixture evenly in the centre of the boned leg of lamb. Roll the meat up tightly and tie securely with string every inch (2·5 cm) or so along the roll.

Position the meat on the spit, testing for a good balance (see p. 50), and cook for about 1½–2 hours or until a meat thermometer placed in the thickest portion registers the required temperature – 185°F (85°C) for well done. Baste occasionally during cooking with the melted butter.

Barbecued Crown Roast   *(Plate 4)*

Serves 6–8

2 best ends of neck
salt and pepper

Stuffing
½ oz (15 g) butter
1 cooking apple, peeled, cored and finely
  chopped

½ lb (250 g) pork sausagemeat
3 tbsp fresh breadcrumbs
1 tsp parsley, finely chopped
1 oz (30 g) walnuts, finely chopped

With a sharp, short-bladed knife, cut through the meat about 1 inch (2·5 cm) from the end of the cutlet bones on each joint. Cut and scrape the fat and meat from the bone ends of both joints. Using a trussing needle and fine string, sew the ends of the joints together back to back (i.e. with the fat inside and the bones curving upwards and outwards).

Melt the butter in a pan and sauté the chopped apple. Add the sausagemeat and combine well with the apple, cooking for 3 minutes. Stir in the remaining ingredients.

Position the crown roast on a piece of extra-thick aluminium foil slightly

T-bone with rosemary (p. 76), honey-wine grilled chicken (p. 97), Christine's barbecued baked beans (p. 116), buttered and grilled corn on the cob (p. 112).

wider than the base of the roast. Place the stuffing in the cavity up to an inch (2·5 cm) or so below the base of the trimmed rib bones to allow the mixture to rise. Cover the tips of the rib bones with foil to prevent charring.

Cook over medium coals by the indirect method allowing 35 minutes per pound (450 g). If the crown roast is cooked unstuffed, allow 30 minutes per pound (450 g).

Spit-roasted Glazed Shoulder of Lamb   *(Plate 5)*

Serves 6–8

3–4 lb (1·4–1·8 kg) shoulder of lamb, boned and rolled
salt and pepper
1 clove garlic (optional)
½ pt (280ml) redcurrant jelly
2 tsp prepared English mustard

Rub the meat with salt and pepper. Slit the surface in several places and insert slivers of garlic if desired. Position the meat on the spit.

Cook over medium coals, allowing 25–30 minutes per pound (450 g) or until a meat thermometer reads 190°F (90°C). During the last 30 minutes of cooking time, baste the lamb shoulder with a glaze made by melting the redcurrant jelly and stirring in the mustard.

Andalusian Lamb Chops

Serves 6

6 lamb chump chops

Marinade
2 tbsp onion, finely chopped
9 tbsp dry sherry
1 bay leaf

½ tsp oregano
¾ tsp basil
3 tbsp tarragon vinegar
6 tbsp oil
½ tsp ground black pepper

Place the chops in a shallow dish. Combine the marinade ingredients and pour over the meat. Marinate overnight in the refrigerator, or for 2–4 hours at room temperature. Turn the chops periodically. If refrigerated, allow the meat to stand at room temperature for about an hour before cooking.

Reserving the marinade, drain the chops well. Set the grill 4–6 inches (10–15 cm) above hot coals and cook for 20–35 minutes. Turn the chops frequently during cooking and baste occasionally with the marinade. Heat the remaining marinade and serve with the chops.

Cinnamon Lamb Cutlets

Serves 6

12 best end lamb cutlets

Marinade
1½ tsp ground cinnamon
1 tbsp brown sugar
3 tbsp oil
6 tbsp orange juice
¼ tsp ground black pepper
¼ tsp salt

Place the cutlets in a shallow dish. Combine the marinade ingredients and pour over the meat. Turn once or twice so that the cutlets are evenly coated. Marinate at room temperature for about 4 hours or overnight in a refrigerator. Turn the cutlets once or twice.

Reserving the marinade, drain the chops and cook over medium hot coals for about 15 minutes, turning occasionally. Baste with the marinade during cooking.

Cumgingon Lamb Kebabs   *(Plate 1)*

Serves 4

1½ lb (0·7 kg) lamb leg steaks
2 tbsp cumin seeds
1 tbsp ground ginger
2 tbsp onion, finely chopped
1 clove garlic, peeled
2 tbsp fresh parsley, chopped

Crush the cumin seeds in a mortar or with the back of a spoon in a teacup. Heat gently in a small, dry, heavy based saucepan for several minutes to release the oils.

Cut the lamb into 1 inch (2·5 cm) cubes and put into a basin with the cumin and the rest of the ingredients. Stir to coat the meat evenly, cover and refrigerate all day or overnight.

Thread the meat on to skewers and cook over medium hot coals, turning and basting from time to time with the fat that drips from the meat.

Garnish with extra parsley and serve in warmed pitta bread.

Spit-roasted Leg of Lamb *(Plate 8)*

Serves 8–10

5–6 lb (2·3–2·7 kg) leg of lamb
4 cloves garlic, sliced
1 tsp salt
½ tsp dried oregano
4 tbsp melted butter
juice of small lemon

Slit the surface of the meat in several places and insert slivers of garlic and a mixture of the salt and oregano. Rub the outside of the meat with any remaining salt and oregano. Insert the spit almost parallel to the bone and place over medium coals.

Mix the melted butter and lemon juice and use to baste the meat a couple of times during the cooking period. The meat is at its best when still slightly pink in the centre (medium rare) and it should take about 1¼–1½ hours. The temperature reading on a meat thermometer will be 140–150°F (60–65°C).

Lamb Kidney Brochette with Sauce Bercy

Serves 4–6

12 lamb kidneys
3 tbsp melted butter

Sauce Bercy
1 tbsp shallots, minced

3 oz (85 g) butter
½ pt (280ml) dry white wine
2 tsp flour
1 tbsp parsley, minced
salt and pepper

Remove the fat and skin from the kidneys and split each from the inside edge to within ½ inch (10 mm) of the outer surface. Extract the white membrane from the inside. Thread on to fine skewers, using a wide stitch across the back of the kidney to hold it in an open position.

Brush the kidneys with half the melted butter and grill over hot coals for about 3 minutes each side, basting occasionally with the remaining butter. Do not be tempted to overcook as the kidneys will rapidly become tough.

Shortly before starting to cook the kidneys, prepare the sauce Bercy. Place the minced shallots and 1 oz (30 g) of the butter in a saucepan and cook until soft. Add the wine and simmer until the liquid has reduced to about half. Mix together the remaining butter and flour and add to the liquid in pan. Continue cooking and stirring until the mixture thickens. Stir in the minced parsley and add salt and pepper to taste.

Serve with the kidneys.

Kidney and Sausage Kebabs *(Plate 1)*

Serves 4

6 oz (170 g) streaky bacon, without rind
4 skinless sausages, cut in half
4 lamb kidneys, skinned, halved and
   cored
4 small tomatoes

Baste
1 tsp tomato purée
1 tsp Worcestershire sauce
1 tbsp oil

Stretch the bacon rashers on a board with the back of a round-bladed knife and cut in half. Roll up each piece and thread on to four skewers, alternating with the sausages, kidneys and tomatoes. Combine the basting ingredients and brush over the kebabs. Place on an oiled grill over medium coals and cook for 10 minutes, turning once. Continue to baste during cooking.

Pineapple Burgers

Serves 6

1 lb (450 g) minced lamb or lean beef
¼ tsp salt
dash of pepper
1 tsp soy sauce
9 oz (255 g) can pineapple slices
2 oz (45 g) brown sugar
2 tsp Worcestershire sauce
6 tbsp tomato ketchup

Place the minced meat, salt, pepper and soy sauce in a bowl and mix well. Shape into 6 burgers. Drain the pineapple, retaining about 2 tbsp of juice. Press a pineapple slice into the surface of each burger and mould the meat around the edges of the slice to hold it firmly during cooking.

    Place the sugar, Worcestershire sauce, pineapple juice and tomato ketchup in a pan and heat gently for a few minutes. Brush the sauce over the burgers and grill over hot coals for about 10 minutes, or until the meat is done and the pineapple is glazed. Baste frequently with sauce during cooking.

Spicy Lamb Kebabs *(Plate 1)*

Serves 4

1½ lb (0·7 kg) leg of lamb, top end
1 green pepper
8 shallots or 2 medium onions
8 button mushrooms

Marinade
¼ pt (140ml) Worcestershire sauce
2 tbsp oil
1 onion, finely chopped
2 tsp sugar
1 tsp salt

Combine the marinade ingredients in a pan with 4 tbsp water, bring to the boil, cover and simmer for 10 minutes. Allow to cool.

Cut the lamb into 1 inch (2·5 cm) cubes, removing any fat. Place the meat in a bowl and pour the marinade over it. Marinate at room temperature for about 4 hours or overnight in a refrigerator, turning the meat over once or twice.

Cut the pepper in half, remove the seeds and cut each half into four. Parboil the shallots or onions. (If medium-sized onions are used, cut each into four pieces.) Reserving the marinade, drain the lamb cubes and thread on to four skewers alternating with the vegetables. Brush with the marinade and place on an oiled grill about 4 inches (10 cm) above hot coals. Cook for about 15 minutes until all sides are browned, turning frequently and basting with the remaining marinade.

Serve with rice, boiled with a pinch of turmeric, and with tomato sauce.

PORK

Hot Cheesy Kebabs

Serves 6

48 cocktail sausages or 1½ inch (4 cm) pieces of frankfurter sausages
4 or 5 eating apples
48 small cubes of Cheddar, Gouda or Gruyère cheese
6 tbsp oil
½ tsp ground cumin
¼ tsp cayenne pepper

Alternately thread a sausage, slice of apple (approximately ¼ inch/6 mm thick) and a cube of cheese on to six skewers until you have eight of each item on each skewer. Keep the sausage, apple and cheese in close contact with each other.

Pork

Grill over medium to hot coals turning from time to time. After about three minutes brush the kebabs with a mixture of oil, cumin and pepper. The kebabs will be ready to serve when the cheese begins to melt and bubble.

Spicy Pork Chops

Serves 6

6 loin chops, 1 inch (2·5 cm) thick
6 tbsp honey
6 tbsp Dijon mustard
¼ tsp chilli powder
¼ tsp salt

Combine the honey, mustard, chilli powder and salt. Spoon the mixture over the pork chops, cover and refrigerate for 4–24 hours.

Reserving the marinade, drain the chops. Place them, thickest ones first, on a lightly greased grill some 4–6 inches (10–15 cm) above hot coals. Cook for 30–40 minutes or until all the pink colour in the centre of the meat has disappeared. Baste occasionally with the marinade during cooking.

Porkyburgers

Serves 6

2 lb (0·9 kg) minced pork
2 eggs, beaten
3 oz (85 g) fresh breadcrumbs
¼ tsp garlic salt
¼ tsp onion salt
2 tbsp oil
¼ tsp ground black pepper
6 soft rolls

Lightly mix together the minced pork, eggs and enough breadcrumbs to give a firm, but not too wet and tacky, mixture. Shape into 6 burgers.

Stir the garlic salt, onion salt and pepper into the oil and brush on one side of the burgers. Cook on the grill over hot coals for approximately 10 minutes, then turn, brush the other side with the seasoned oil and cook for a further 10 minutes or until nicely browned. Toast the rolls during the last few minutes of cooking and serve with the burgers.

Paprika Pork Chops

Serves 6

6 pork rib or loin chops 1 inch (2·5 cm) thick
1 tsp paprika
1 tsp rosemary, crushed
¼ tsp ground black pepper
3 tbsp oil

Wipe the chops and slash the fat around the edge of each at ½ inch (1 cm) intervals. Stir the paprika, rosemary and black pepper into the oil and brush both sides of the chops thoroughly with the mixture. Allow to stand for 1 hour.

Cook the chops over medium to hot coals for 15–20 minutes on each side, until well done.

Pork Saté with Indonesian Sauce

Serves 6

2 lb (0·9 kg) boneless pork loin
6 tbsp chutney
1 tbsp soy sauce
3 tbsp tomato ketchup
½ tsp chilli powder
2 tbsp oil
Indonesian Sauce (see p. 124)

Finely chop the chutney (or purée in a blender). Place in a mixing bowl with the soy sauce, tomato, chilli powder and oil. Cut the meat into 1 inch (2·5 cm) squares (about ¾ inch/2 cm thick) and marinate in the mixture for about 4 hours, turning occasionally.

Prepare the Indonesian Sauce and allow to stand for at least 2 hours before use.

Impale the meat pieces on six skewers, or bamboo sticks, and cook over hot coals for about 12 minutes, ensuring that all sides of the meat are browned.

Reheat the sauce gently and serve with the saté.

Spit-roasted Boned Leg of Pork

Serves 6–8

1 leg of pork, boned (allow about 6–8 oz/170–225 g per person)

Marinade
1 pt (600ml) cider
4 tbsp lemon juice
4 tbsp orange juice
4 tbsp wine vinegar
½ tsp garlic salt
½ tsp onion salt
¼ tsp ground black pepper or cayenne pepper

Combine the marinade ingredients and pour over the leg of pork. Leave overnight.

Reserving the marinade, drain the leg, score evenly and position it on the spit. Brush the meat well with the marinade and cook slowly over medium coals, allowing about 25 minutes per pound (450 g), or until a meat thermometer reads 190°F (90°C). Baste the meat frequently with the marinade during cooking. Place a drip pan under the meat to catch the juices, and use them to make gravy.

Glazed Roast Loin of Pork

Serves 6–8

approx. 4 lb (1·8 kg) loin of pork
4 fl. oz (110ml) apple juice
2 tbsp soy sauce
1 clove garlic, minced or pressed
¼ tsp ground ginger

Position the loin on the lightly greased food grill, fat side up. Place lid on barbecue and cook over medium hot coals.

Combine the apple juice, soy sauce, garlic and ground ginger. After the meat has been cooking for 1 hour, baste it with this mixture. Replace the lid and cook for a further 1½ hours, basting frequently, or until meat thermometer, inserted into thickest area of the muscle, registers 190°F (90°C).

Roast Loin of Pork with Ambrosia Stuffing

Serves 6–8

4 lb (1·8 kg) pork loin, boned and rolled

Ambrosia stuffing
3 tbsp butter
2 medium onions, chopped
2 apples, cored, peeled and chopped

6 oz (170 g) ripe olives, chopped
3 oz (85 g) walnuts, chopped
¼ tsp dried thyme
½ tsp salt
3 oz (85 g) soft breadcrumbs
3 tbsp melted butter
3 oz (85 g) ham, chopped

Using a sharp knife, slice the roast halfway down at 1 inch (2·5 cm) intervals. Continue each slice to form deep pockets, leaving a 1 inch (2·5 cm) wall on the sides and bottom.

Heat the butter in a skillet and sauté the onions, stirring occasionally until they are limp and transparent. Add the chopped apple and cook for 1 minute. Add the remaining ingredients and mix well.

Generously stuff the roast, then tie lengthwise at 1 inch (2·5 cm) intervals to hold it firmly together.

Cook for 1½–2 hours until meat thermometer, buried halfway in the centre slice of the roast, registers 190°F (90°C). Remove from barbecue and allow to stand for 10 minutes before carving. Remove the string and slice through the meat between pockets to yield individually stuffed portions.

Friends tell me that this dish tastes equally delightful when cold, and it is one to impress friends with at semi-formal barbecue parties.

Smoky Mountain Ribs

Serves 4–6

6 lb (2·7 kg) lean spare-ribs
2 tbsp 'liquid smoke' (optional)
2 tsp salt
½ pt (280 ml) tomato ketchup
2 fl. oz (60 ml) wine vinegar

4 oz (100 g) brown sugar
2 tbsp Worcestershire sauce
1 tsp chilli powder
½ tsp ground black pepper
½ tsp celery seed

Cut ribs into four-rib sections. If 'liquid smoke' is available use it to brush both sides of rib sections and then refrigerate for 30 minutes. Arrange ribs in a rib rack or shallow roasting pan and sprinkle with salt. Place the pan in the centre of the cooking grill.

Cover barbecue and cook ribs for about 1¾ hours or until they are tender and nicely browned.

Combine the remaining ingredients and mix well. Brush over the ribs several times during last 45 minutes of cooking.

Serve with the remaining sauce which can be heated if desired.

Sweet and Sour Spare-ribs   *(Plate 3)*

Serves 6–10

4–6 lb (1·8–2·7 kg) lean spare-ribs

Sweet and sour sauce
1 tsp salt
3 tbsp soy sauce
3 tbsp oil

¼ pt (140 ml) wine vinegar
5 oz (140 g) brown sugar
6 tbsp pineapple juice
1 tsp fresh ginger, grated or ¼ tsp
   powdered ginger

Rub the spare-ribs thoroughly with salt. Then place directly on to the grill, or thread them on to the spit. The grill should be raised to approximately 6 inches (15 cm) above medium coals and the ribs turned every 10 minutes.

Combine the rest of the ingredients with 6 tbsp water and brush the mixture over the ribs after 30–40 minutes of cooking. Cook for a further 30–40 minutes or until the ribs are done (the meat should pull away from the end of the rib bones). Basting and turning should be a continuous process to ensure even flavouring and to prevent the ribs becoming charred.

Serve with a pineapple garnish and, if desired, an additional sweet and sour sauce (see p. 123).

Spiced Orange Glazed Spare-ribs   *(Plate 3)*

Serves 4

3 lb (1·4 kg) meaty spare-ribs

Marinade and glaze
2 tbsp clear honey
juice of ½ lemon

grated rind of ½ orange
juice of 2 oranges
2 tbsp Worcestershire sauce
1 tsp soy sauce
salt

Combine the marinade ingredients in a pan and heat gently. Simmer for 2 minutes and allow to cool. Cut the spare-ribs into serving pieces and place in a shallow dish. Pour over the marinade and refrigerate for 12–24 hours, turning occasionally.

Reserving the marinade, drain the spare-ribs and place in a roasting pan.

Roast the spare-ribs at 350°F (180°C), gas mark 4, for 1 hour. When required, place them on an oiled grill about 4 inches (10 cm) above hot coals. Cook for about 12–15 minutes until well glazed and crisp, turning frequently and basting with the marinade.

Jeannie's Pork and Apricot Kebabs

Serves 4

1 lb (450 g) pork fillet
8 shallots or 2 medium onions
8 oz (225 g) can of apricot halves
6 oz (170 g) soft brown sugar
4 tbsp apricot jam
6 tbsp wine vinegar
1 tsp dry mustard
4 tbsp Worcestershire sauce
salt and pepper

Cut the pork fillet into 1 inch (2·5 cm) cubes. Parboil shallots for about 5 minutes. If using medium-sized onions parboil whole for about 6 to 7 minutes, then cut into quarters. Drain apricot halves, reserving juice. Alternately thread pork cubes, apricot halves and shallots, or onion pieces, on to skewers.

Combine the rest of the ingredients in a pan and heat gently to dissolve the sugar. Brush the kebabs with the mixture, place them on a greased grill and cook over medium to hot coals for about 15 minutes, turning and basting with the mixture several times during cooking.

Barbecued Sucking Pig

Serves 8–10

15 lb (6·8 kg) sucking pig, cleaned
3 small oranges
2 oz (55 g) coarse salt
2 bay leaves
1 lime (optional)

Marinade
6 tbsp soy sauce
2 tbsp dry sherry
4 tbsp oil
2 oz (55 g) brown sugar
1½ tsp salt
½ tsp ground black pepper
2 cloves garlic

Wash the pig under cold running water and pat dry, inside and out, with kitchen paper. Combine the marinade ingredients, mix well and allow to stand for about 30 minutes. Brush the entire cavity and outer skin of the pig with the mixture and leave for 2–3 hours before repeating the exercise. Cut the oranges in half, squeeze out the juice and put to one side. Place the orange skins in the pig's cavity with the bay leaves and scatter over with the coarse salt. Sew up the body and neck cavities using a trussing needle and string.

Stuff the lime (a block of wood or compressed ball of aluminium foil will suffice) into the pig's mouth to hold the jaws open during cooking. Cover the ears, front feet, nose and tail with extra-thick foil to prevent scorching – it will need tying on or pinning with wooden cocktail sticks. The foil should be removed about 30 minutes before cooking is completed. Bring rear legs of pig forward under its body and hold in position with strong twine. Push the spit, from the tail end, through the body cavity so that it emerges from the mouth. Firmly secure the spit-forks using a pair of pliers. Bring the pig's front legs forward under its head and tie to the spit-fork with strong twine.

The cooking technique to be followed will depend upon the equipment available, but whether you are using a barbecue of the type featured on p. 11, a large covered barbecue or simply a basic brick-built structure with a hand-operated spit, it will be necessary to arrange the coals in such a way that a drip pan can be positioned to catch the fat. Half filling the drip pan with liquid will prevent the drippings from over-heating and igniting.

Cooking time will vary according to the technique being followed, but a 15 lb (6·8 kg) pig should take approximately 4 hours (allow about 25 minutes per pound (450 g) for a 20 lb/9·1 kg pig). Check it is ready by inserting a meat thermometer in the thickest muscle of a hind leg just prior to the completion of the estimated cooking time. The thermometer should register 170°F (75°C). Fully cooked, the meat will have a light yellow/white colour – there should be no trace of pink in any juices coming from the meat.

Brush the pig with the reserved marinade two or three times during the first two hours of cooking. Add the reserved orange juice to the marinade and baste with this mixture two or three times during the final period of cooking. Let the pig stand for 20–30 minutes before carving.

When carving, first separate the hind and fore legs from one side before cutting off the complete loin. Carve the loin into serving pieces and repeat on the other side.

Sancages

Many different kinds of sausages are now obtainable from most delicatessens. We are, in fact, in danger of becoming a little blasé about them now that we have easy access to the tasty exotica of Italy, Germany, Poland, Switzerland and France.

Black pudding and frankfurters are almost old hat although few perhaps have yet experienced the delight of barbecued black pudding. Sausages have always been big business, but nowadays they have taken on the sort of mystique that one associates with real ale. Each town boasts a butcher who prides himself on his 'Saturday morning specials'. Many butchers actually set out to produce the perfect barbecue banger, i.e. one *almost* guaranteed to cook without flare-up. Those readers with a sausage-making accessory on their food mixer should certainly have a go at making a Cumberland sausage with its giant Catherine-wheel shape (not only tasty, but very pretty into the bargain).

Some sausages, e.g. bratwurst, are best gently simmered in water for about 10 minutes or so before grilling over low to medium coals. Slow and gentle grilling is in fact all that is needed for most continental sausages.

The cooking technique required when cooking a fresh meat sausage varies from sausage to sausage. Some will keep their shape and not burst when grilled over hot charcoal while others need to be pricked before cooking to allow the fat to drain off. When cooking a large quantity of pork sausages I find it helps considerably if the sausages are piled up and cooked by the indirect method (using a covered barbecue) before I direct grill them. The large amount of fat sweated out of the sausages greatly reduces the possibility of flare-up (this tip also applies to burgers).

An easy way to produce bite-size sausage appetizers is to cut chipolatas into 1–1½ inch (2·5–4 cm) sections and thread these, with a ½ inch (1 cm) gap, on to long skewers. When cooked through it is a simple matter to shove the sausage pieces off on to a serving plate. Pushing a skewer down the full length of a long sausage will prevent it from curling up.

VEAL

Stuffed Veal Cutlets

Serves 4

4 veal cutlets
4 very thin slices of bacon
4 slices Gruyère cheese
oil
salt and pepper
grated nutmeg

Cut a deep pocket into the thickness of each cutlet. Slide a slice of bacon and a slice of Gruyère into each pocket. Coat the outside of the cutlets with oil and sprinkle with the salt, pepper and grated nutmeg.

Grill the cutlets over medium hot coals for 4–6 minutes, turning once, until the cheese begins to melt and run from inside the cutlets. Serve immediately.

Spicy Veal Kebabs

Serves 4

1 lb (450 g) lean veal
6 rashers streaky bacon
8 oz (225 g) button mushrooms
1 green pepper, chopped
salt and pepper
pinch ground ginger
pinch ground mace
pinch ground nutmeg
3 oz (85 g) butter

Cut the veal into cubes. Roll up each rasher of bacon and cut in half to make 2 rolls. Thread the bacon, veal, mushrooms and green pepper on to skewers, making sure that the bacon is next to the veal. Sprinkle the meat with the seasonings and spices. Dot with butter. Cook over medium coals until the bacon and veal are cooked.

Serve with a green salad.

Skewered Veal and Ham Olives

Serves 4

4 veal escalopes, cut into thin 4–5 inch (10–12·5 cm) squares
lemon juice
salt and pepper
4 thin slices cooked ham (approximately the same size as the veal escalopes)

4 rashers streaky bacon, thinly sliced
2 medium onions, cut into ¼ inch (6 mm) thick slices
sage leaves
2 tbsp melted bacon fat or dripping

Season the veal escalopes with the lemon juice, salt and pepper. Lay a slice of ham on each escalope. Roll up the meat and tightly wrap a piece of streaky bacon around each package. Thread the olives on to skewers (two per skewer) alternating with a slice of onion and a sage leaf. Pour melted bacon fat, or dripping, over the olives and cook over medium to hot coals for about 8 minutes or until cooked through. Turn and baste three or four times during cooking.

POULTRY and GAME

Chicken à l'Avocado

Serves 4

2 whole chicken breasts
¼ pt (140 ml) dry white wine
3 fl. oz (90 ml) oil
2 cloves garlic, crushed
½ tsp salt
2 ripe medium avocados
2 small hard-boiled eggs, shelled
juice 1 lemon

Neville's sauce
¼ pt (140 ml) mayonnaise
2 tbsp clear honey
1 tbsp Dijon mustard
3 fl. oz (90 ml) oil
2 oz (55 g) onion, finely chopped
1 tsp parsley, minced
juice ½ lemon

Remove the skin from each chicken breast and bone carefully, keeping the breast in one piece. Place breasts on a board, cut side up, cover with greaseproof paper and, using a wooden rolling pin or meat hammer, beat out thinly. Combine the wine, oil, garlic and salt in a shallow bowl. Immerse the breasts in the mixture and leave to marinate for approximately 30 minutes.

Combine all the sauce ingredients and blend well. Put to one side.

Cut each avocado in half lengthwise, remove the pit and pare off the tough outer skin. Bathe the flesh completely in lemon juice. Place an egg in the recess left by the pit and cover with the other half of the avocado. Drain the chicken breasts, reserving the marinade, pat dry and wrap each around a re-assembled pear. Secure with wooden cocktail sticks which have already been soaked in water.

Cook the chicken packages over medium hot coals for about 30 minutes, or until the meat is firm and springy. Turn the breasts frequently during cooking, basting on each turn with the reserved marinade.

After cooking let the stuffed breasts stand for 10–12 minutes before cutting in halves lengthwise. Pour the sauce over the portions.

Honey-wine Grilled Chicken *(Plate 6)*

Serves 4

4 chicken quarters

Marinade
4 tbsp soy sauce
¼ pt (140 ml) white wine
¼ pt (140 ml) orange juice

4 tbsp clear honey
1 tsp prepared English mustard
¼ tsp ground allspice
1 tsp paprika
1 clove garlic, crushed

Combine all the marinade ingredients with 2 tbsp water and pour over the chicken pieces. (If using frozen chicken, make sure that the pieces have thawed properly.) Leave for 2–4 hours, turning several times.

Reserving the marinade, drain the chicken pieces and cook over medium hot coals until both sides are cooked through and golden brown. Check if they are ready by piercing the thickest part of the joint with a skewer – if the juices run clear the chicken is cooked but if any pinkness is apparent cook a little longer. Baste with the marinade several times during cooking.

Richard's Streaky Chicken Drumsticks

Serves 4

8 chicken drumsticks
3 oz (85 g) cream cheese
salt and pepper
8 rashers streaky bacon
melted butter or oil

Using a sharp, short-bladed knife make an incision into the fattest part of the muscle of each drumstick and fill the slit with the cream cheese. After seasoning, wrap a rasher of bacon around each drumstick. Secure the bacon with wooden cocktail sticks which have already been soaked in water.

Cook over medium hot coals for 5–6 minutes each side, basting frequently with the butter or oil.

Orange Burgundy Duckling

Serves 4

4½ lb (2 kg) duckling
½ pt (280 ml) Burgundy wine
1 tsp salt
¼ tsp ground black pepper
¼ tsp thyme
1 orange, quartered
2 slices onion
1 celery top (washed)
generous ¼ pt (140 ml) concentrated orange juice

Remove the giblets from the duckling. Wash and pat dry, inside and out, with absorbent kitchen paper.

Brush the cavity of the duckling with a small amount of the Burgundy and sprinkle with salt, pepper and thyme. Stuff with the orange quarters, onion slices and celery top; close the cavity with skewers.

Combine the remaining Burgundy with the orange juice and brush the outside of the duck with it. Cover the barbecue and roast the duckling for 2–2¼ hours or until tender. After 30 minutes prick the skin of the thigh and breast areas with a large needle and baste with the wine and orange mixture. Baste frequently during roasting.

Discard the contents of the cavity before serving.

Duckling with Orange-soy Glaze

Serves 4

4½ lb (2 kg) duckling
¼ tsp thyme
1 tsp salt
3 tbsp soy sauce
6 tbsp orange juice
1½ tsp honey
⅛ tsp ground black pepper
Spicy Orange Sauce (see p. 124)

Remove the giblets from the duck. Wash and pat dry, inside and out, with absorbent kitchen paper.

Sprinkle the cavity of the duckling with the thyme and salt. Truss the duckling as compactly as possible and push the spit in from a point just in front of the tail (through the bone) to exit, again through the bone, near the apex of the wish-bone. (The spit will therefore be inserted diagonally through the body of the duckling.)

Combine the soy sauce, honey and pepper and warm in a small pot or container. Spit-roast the duckling for 1½–2 hours or until tender. Brush the warm glaze on to the duckling two or three times during the first hour or so of cooking and again two or three times during the last 25 minutes.

Serve with Spicy Orange Sauce.

Note

During the early part of cooking the fat from the duckling will run freely. To avoid the problem of flare-up it is therefore essential to use a drip pan and follow the prescribed spit-roasting technique as featured on pp. 49–50. Part-cooking the duckling in advance will considerably reduce the amount of fat and help ensure that the meat is cooked right through (essential with all poultry).

Spit-roasted Turkey Roll

Serves 20–25

4½ lb (2 kg) sweet-cured turkey roll
Herb Butter (see p. 126)

Remove the casing from the turkey roll. Lightly scratch the surface with the prongs of a fork. Mount the roll on the spit, securing in place with the spit-forks. Cook with the spit set about 6–9 inches (15–23 cm) over medium hot coals for about 10 minutes per pound (450 g) or until the internal temperature registers around 120°F (50°C).

Baste the meat three or four times during cooking with the herb butter. Allow to rest for 15–20 minutes before carving into even-sized steaks.

Note

Sausages or meat rolls that are 4–6 inches (10–15 cm) in diameter, e.g. Mortadella, will take 40–50 minutes to heat through, while those that are less than 4 inches (10 cm) in diameter should take only 25–30 minutes.

Devilled Drumsticks

Serves 6

12 chicken drumsticks

Marinade
1 tbsp curry powder (mild or hot to taste)
1 tbsp Dijon mustard
2 tbsp tomato ketchup

1 tsp castor sugar
2 tbsp Worcestershire sauce
¼ pt (140 ml) oil
⅛ tsp paprika
salt and pepper

Score each drumstick with a sharp pointed knife, cutting to the bone in several places. Combine the marinade ingredients and mix well. Pour over the drumsticks and rub the mixture into the deep cuts. Leave for 4–6 hours or refrigerate overnight.

Reserving the marinade, drain the drumsticks and cook over medium to hot coals for about 30 minutes. Turn the drumsticks from time to time while they are cooking and baste with the marinade.

Sesame Chicken Drumsticks

Serves 4

8 chicken drumsticks

Marinade
1 clove garlic, minced
1 tsp grated ginger root
2 tbsp sesame seed
2 tsp sesame oil
¼ tsp cayenne pepper
1 oz (30 g) spring onion, minced

Wash the drumsticks and pat dry. Combine the marinade ingredients, pour over the drumsticks and mix well. Refrigerate for 2–3 hours.

Reserving the marinade, drain and cook the drumsticks over medium to hot coals for 30 minutes, or until nicely browned and cooked through. Turn the drumsticks from time to time while they are cooking and baste with the marinade.

Honey Crunchy Turkey Drumsticks

Serves 6

6 small turkey drumsticks
1 tbsp lemon juice
3 tbsp clear honey
4 tbsp demerara sugar
salt and pepper

Wash the drumsticks and pat dry; pierce each all over with the point of a skewer.

Combine the lemon juice and honey in a small saucepan and heat gently. Brush the mixture over the drumsticks, sprinkle with demerara sugar and season with salt and pepper.

Cook the drumsticks over medium to hot coals for about 30–35 minutes or until cooked through and golden brown with a crisp, crunchy coating.

Tandoori Chicken

Serves 4

3 lb (1·4 kg) chicken
1 small onion
4 cloves garlic
½ inch (1 cm) piece of fresh ginger root,
    peeled and chopped
1 tsp cumin
1 tsp coriander
½ tsp chilli powder
½ tsp cinnamon
1 tsp salt
¼ pt (140 ml) yoghurt
juice 1 lemon

Tandoori basting sauce
3 oz (85 g) butter, melted
½ tsp nutmeg
½ tsp cinnamon
½ tsp coriander
2 tbsp lemon juice

Combine all the Tandoori basting sauce ingredients and blend well: put to one side.

Pierce the chicken all over with the point of a skewer. Grind the onion, garlic and ginger together in a blender. Add spices and seasoning and mix thoroughly. Beat the yoghurt in a bowl until smooth; blend in the spice paste and lemon juice. Rub the mixture on the chicken and let it marinate in the refrigerator for at least 4 hours or overnight.

Cook the chicken for approximately 1½ hours or until juices run clear when chicken thigh is pierced with a skewer. Baste frequently during cooking with the Tandoori basting sauce.

Buttered Breast of Turkey

Serves 4 as a
main course, or
12 as an
appetizer

2 turkey breasts, 1 lb (450 g) each
3 oz (85 g) softened butter
salt and pepper
peanut oil for basting

Discard the skin from the turkey breasts. Slice each across into two pieces. Place on a board, cut side up, cover with greaseproof paper and, using a wooden rolling pin or meat hammer, beat out thinly. Cover the surface of the meat with the butter, sprinkle salt and pepper to taste and roll into a cylindrical shape. Tie with fine string in three places. Rub the surface of each roll with butter, and season again to taste.

Cook until 'fork tender' or a meat thermometer inserted into the centre of a roll registers 190°F (90°C). Baste frequently with peanut oil.

Stuffed Buttered Breast of Turkey

Here are a few suggestions for fillings:

1. Add 1 clove garlic, crushed, and 1 tsp dried fennel weed to the softened butter.
2. Sauté chopped onions and sliced mushrooms and mix them, together with chopped parsley, into the softened butter.
3. Roll the buttered turkey breast around a fat cooked pork sausage.
4. Spread your favourite poultry stuffing over the buttered turkey breast before rolling.

Note

Lay slices of streaky bacon over the rolls to help make them self-basting.

Tipsy Turkey

Serves 6–8

8–10 lb (3·6–4·5 kg) turkey
salt and pepper
oil (peanut or vegetable), melted butter
   or margarine

Tipsy sauce
½ tsp marjoram
¼ tsp ground black pepper
½ tsp salt

2 tsp brown sugar
2 tsp onion, minced
1 tsp French mustard
pinch of thyme
¼ pt (140 ml) sherry
⅛ pt (75 ml) oil

Mix all the sauce ingredients together and stir vigorously. Put to one side (the sauce will require a further vigorous stir or shake before use).

Clean the turkey; sprinkle the cavity generously with salt and pepper. Lock the wings behind the back or fasten next to the breast and tie securely. Tie the legs and tail together (some oven-ready birds will already have their legs secured by a band of skin). Insert a meat thermometer into thickest portion of the thigh, ensuring that its point is not touching a bone.

Centre the turkey on a greased cooking grill directly over the drip pan, which should itself be centred on the lower charcoal grill. Brush the bird lightly all over with the oil, butter or margarine. Place the cover on the barbecue and cook to a temperature of 190°F (90°C) or until the juices run clear when the thigh is pierced with a skewer. Cooking time will vary depending upon which type of covered barbecue is used, but an 8–10 lb (3·6–4·5 kg) bird should cook in 2½–3½ hours. Baste periodically with the sauce during cooking to give the bird a delicious golden glaze. The earlier and more often the sauce is applied, the darker the colour and the more distinctive the 'tipsy' flavour. Add charcoal as required during the cooking period to maintain the temperature. If the turkey is stuffed at the neck, allow 3–5 minutes additional cooking time per pound (450 g).

Barbecued Pheasant

Serves 2–4

1 plump pheasant, well hung
3 tbsp butter
3 slices streaky bacon
ground black pepper

Carefully wipe the pheasant inside and out with a damp cloth. Cover the wing tips and the knuckle end of the legs with foil. Spread a generous layer of butter over the outside of the bird and wrap around with the slices of bacon. Season with the ground pepper.

Cook, using the indirect method, in a covered barbecue (with the charcoal at medium heat) for 1–1¼ hours. Remove the bacon during the last 15 minutes to allow the breast to brown nicely.

Barbecued Quail

Serves 4

12 quail, drawn and split lengthwise
   through the breast-bone
4 oz (115 g) melted butter or oil

Marinade
1 pt (600 ml) dry white wine
3 tbsp lemon juice

1½ tbsp wine vinegar
2 cloves garlic, crushed
1 tsp dried whole tarragon or rosemary
   leaves
1 bay leaf
1 tsp salt
¼ tsp ground black pepper

Combine the marinade ingredients in a saucepan and heat until simmering. Remove the pan from the heat, cover and allow to stand for about 1½ hours before adding the quail to the mixture. Refrigerate for about 6–8 hours or overnight.

Remove the quail from the marinade, drain and then pat dry. Grill the quail, initially cut side down, for about 15–20 minutes over medium hot coals, turning from time to time and basting frequently with the melted butter until they are nicely browned.

FISH and SHELLFISH

Grilled Mussels

Serves 4

40–50 mussels
large bunch dried herbs (rosemary, thyme, etc.)

Scrape, scrub and wash mussels carefully. Place them on the grill about 6 inches (15 cm) above medium hot coals. Scatter the dried herbs on the coals throughout the short cooking period. When the mussels have opened fully, leave them on the grill for another minute and then serve immediately. Discard any that have failed to open.

Grilled Fish Fillets with Almonds

Serves 6

2 lb (0.9 kg) fish fillets
4 tbsp softened butter or margarine
½ tsp salt
⅛ tsp ground black pepper
pinch ground nutmeg
pinch paprika
pinch onion powder
2 tbsp almonds, blanched and slivered
2 tbsp lemon juice
2 tbsp parsley, finely chopped

If using frozen fish fillets, thaw sufficiently to separate them. Brush both sides of the fillets with about half the softened butter or margarine. Combine all the seasonings and sprinkle over the fish.

Grease the grill bars or hinged wire basket, if you have one, and cook the fish – skin side down – about 4–6 inches (10–15 cm) above medium hot coals for about 5 minutes. Turn and cook for a further five minutes or until the fish is easily flaked with a fork.

Sauté the almonds in the remaining butter, using a foil drip pan (see p. 61), until golden brown, then stir in the lemon juice. Spoon the almonds and lemon–butter mixture over the fish. Sprinkle with the chopped parsley and serve immediately.

Neville's Mushroom and Scallop Kebabs *(Plate 1)*

Makes 12
appetizers

12 scallops
12 mushroom caps (large buttons)
6 tbsp melted butter
juice of 1 lemon
salt and pepper

Remove the scallops from their shells and halve any large ones across the grain. Rinse the scallops and mushrooms, pat dry. Place a scallop in each mushroom cap and push a skewer through the centre of the cap and scallop to hold them securely in place. Assemble four or six scallops and mushrooms on each skewer leaving a gap of 1 inch (2·5 cm) or so between them. Brush generously with melted butter and sprinkle over with the lemon juice, salt and pepper.

Grill the kebabs over medium hot coals for 8–10 minutes or until the scallops have become opaque and firm to the touch. Turn and baste frequently during cooking with the melted butter.

Red Mullet Grilled with Fennel *(Plate 2)*

Serves 4

4 large or 8 small red mullet

Marinade
1 tbsp melted butter
2 tbsp oil
½ tsp peppercorns, cracked

3 large bay leaves, each broken into 4
   pieces
2 tbsp dry white wine
2 cloves garlic, finely chopped
1 tbsp chopped fennel leaves

Clean the fish, but leave the liver (considered a great delicacy) intact. Mix together the marinade ingredients and pour over the fish. Marinate for about 1 hour.

Reserving the marinade, drain the fish and cook for 5–8 minutes on each side, depending upon the size of the fish. Baste two or three times during cooking with the marinade.

Grilled Sprats

Serves 4

1 ½ lb (0·7 kg) sprats
3 tbsp oil
3 oz (85 g) seasoned flour
lemon wedges
4 tbsp chopped parsley

Clean sprats, if desired, by making a small incision behind the gill of each fish and gently squeezing the belly towards the incision. When expelling the gut try to keep the fish head intact. Wash the fish well and pat dry with kitchen paper. Toss the fish in seasoned flour and lightly brush with oil.

Place the fish on a well-oiled grill and cook over hot coals for approximately 5 minutes. Turn once and lightly coat with oil. Serve garnished with lemon and a sprinkling of chopped parsley.

Note

Most fish cooked on an open barbecue can be awkward to handle during cooking. In addition, the small fry, like sprats, can easily fall through the grill bars. A long-handled hinged wire basket (broiler), providing the wires are closely spaced together, will overcome both problems in an efficient and speedy way. Oil the inside of the basket before placing the fish inside.

Marinated Fish Steaks

Serves 4

4 fresh or frozen halibut or haddock steaks 1–1 ½ inches (2·5–4 cm) thick
Seafare Marinade (see p. 124)
3 oz (85 g) butter, melted
½ tsp salt
¼ tsp ground black pepper
1 tbsp lemon juice

Place the fish in a shallow dish, pour the marinade over them and allow to stand for about 30 minutes, turning once.

Tear off four pieces of 18 inch (46 cm) heavy-duty aluminium foil and brush melted butter on the polished surface of each piece. Drain the fish and place one portion on each of the buttered surfaces; sprinkle with salt and pepper. Combine the remainder of the melted butter with the lemon juice and brush over the fish. Fold the foil over and secure the edges tightly.

Place the packages on the grill over medium coals and cook for approximately 20 minutes or until the fish flakes easily with a fork. Open the foil during the last 5 minutes of cooking time to allow the barbecue smoke to flavour the fish.

Herring Grilled with Fennel

Serves 4

4 medium herrings
4 oz (115 g) butter
¼ tsp ground cardamom
½ tsp ground coriander seed
½ tsp salt
⅛ tsp ground black pepper
2 tbsp lemon juice
½ pt (280 ml) yoghurt
sprigs of fresh fennel or dill or thyme

Scrape the fish to remove all the scales. Remove the heads, trim the tails, gut and wash the fish well. Make three diagonal cuts across each side of the body. Dry fish on paper towelling.

Melt the butter in a small saucepan and add all the other ingredients, except the fennel. Brush the fish inside and out with the mixture.

Place the fish in a flat hinged wire basket (broiler) that has been greased on the inside. Alternatively, place them directly on to a well-greased grill and cook over hot coals, turning and basting frequently, for about 25 minutes. During the last ten minutes or so of cooking, place the sprigs of fresh herbs on the coals.

Heat any remaining sauce and serve with the fish.

Barbecued Salmon Steaks *(Plate 2)*

Serves 4

4 salmon steaks about 1 inch (2·5 cm) thick
salt and ground white pepper
1 tsp onion, minced
½ tsp paprika
generous pinch of garlic salt
2 tsp lemon juice

Wipe the fish with a damp cloth. Season both sides of the salmon steaks with salt and pepper. Stir the minced onion, paprika, garlic salt and some more pepper to taste, into the lemon juice. Brush both sides of the salmon steaks with the mixture and allow them to stand for about 25 minutes.

Cook over medium coals for 6–7 minutes each side, basting frequently with any left-over marinade.

Stuffed Trout

Serves 4

4 trout, 8–10 oz (225–285 g) each
4 oz (115 g) walnuts, finely chopped
2 tbsp lemon juice
2 tbsp parsley, minced
½ tsp salt
1 egg
1 tbsp oil
lemon wedges

Clean the trout, keeping the head and tail intact. Wash thoroughly and pat dry with kitchen paper.

Mix the walnuts, lemon juice, parsley and salt together and bind with the beaten egg. Stuff each of the fish with the mixture (about 3 tbsp per fish) and close the openings with fine metal skewers or cocktail sticks. Brush oil on both sides of the fish and place on an oiled grill positioned 5–6 inches (12–15 cm) above hot coals. Cook for about 6 minutes each side or until the flesh can be easily flaked with a fork.

Serve with lemon wedges.

Grilled Sardines with Herb Butter   *(Plate 2)*

Serves 4–6

16 fresh sardines
3 tbsp oil
salt and pepper
Herb Butter (see p. 128)

Clean the fish, pat dry and brush lightly with oil. Season to taste with salt and pepper. Place the fish on a well-oiled grill and cook over hot coals for approximately 10 minutes, turning once.

Serve with pats of herb butter.

Note

Frozen sardines may be used, but thaw before cooking.

Cheesy Crusted Mackerel

Serves 4

4 mackerel, ¾ lb (340 g) each
1 oz (30 g) dry white breadcrumbs
2 oz (55 g) Parmesan cheese, grated
2 cloves garlic, minced
¼ tsp salt

⅛ tsp ground black pepper
4 tbsp oil
4 tbsp lemon juice
1 tbsp parsley, chopped
½ tsp dried basil

Clean and bone the mackerel and, if desired, remove the heads. Combine breadcrumbs, Parmesan cheese, 1 clove of garlic, salt and pepper and mix thoroughly.

Prepare a basting sauce by mixing together the salad oil, lemon juice, chopped parsley, basil and remaining clove of garlic.

Dip each fish fillet in the basting sauce and then into the cheese and crumb mixture. Place the fish, flesh side down, on a well-oiled grill over medium coals and cook for about 5 minutes. Turn the fish over and brush the basting sauce over the upper side. Continue grilling and basting occasionally for a further 8–10 minutes or until the skin is crisp and the flesh can easily be flaked with a fork.

VEGETABLES AND FRUIT

Barbecuing does for vegetables what English mustard does for roast beef – it enhances the flavour and helps to rekindle the appetite. For many people, unfortunately, years of over-boiling vegetables and then pouring half their flavour (and nutritional value) down the waste-pipe along with the hot water have resulted in an acceptance of blandness. However, for those who still have discerning taste buds, revitalized perhaps by the tantalizing flavour of meat grilled over charcoal, eating vegetables cooked in the manner described below will be a rewarding experience.

Most vegetables, and fruit for that matter, can be cooked directly on the grill over a moderate heat; they will require frequent basting with butter or a made-up basting sauce. Some vegetables need to be wrapped in a loose, but secure, packet of aluminium foil so that they can cook in their own juices – or in a little water.

Cooking Fresh or Frozen Vegetables in Foil

Plate 7 shows a representative selection of vegetables suitable for cooking in foil. Included in the selection are carrots, runner beans, peas with mushroom slices, asparagus spears, sliced courgettes, broccoli, Brussels sprouts and broad beans; small whole onions are also suitable.

Two layers of extra-thick aluminium foil, 12 inches (30 cm) square, should comfortably accommodate up to 3 or 4 portions of most vegetables. The edges of the foil should be raised slightly before placing the cleaned and prepared vegetables in the centre. Season as desired with salt and pepper, add 1 tbsp water and dot the vegetables with a 'nugget' of butter or margarine (a level tbsp should suffice). Alternatively, use one of the flavoured butters on pp. 127–8. The package should be closed by bringing together and double folding the top and end edges of the foil. Make sure that the end lapping is slightly raised in order to prevent any juices from leaking from the package and that a little space is left under the top fold to allow for steam expansion.

Cooking vegetables in this way lends itself to covered barbecues where the indirect method of cooking can be employed. However, when cooking directly over charcoal it will be necessary to turn the packages over occasionally, thus making it essential that all joints are leakproof. Avoid cooking foil-wrapped vegetables (other than potatoes) directly over high heat.

The best results will be obtained with a moderate heat and the grill set 6–10 inches (15–25 cm) above the fire-bed. A time-chart for cooking foil-wrapped fresh and frozen vegetables appears on p. 133.

Buttered and Grilled Corn on the Cob   *(Plate 6)*

1 ear of young sweet corn per person
softened butter
salt

Method 3
Garlic Butter (see p. 127)

Method 4
1 rasher fat bacon per person

Method 1

Strip away the husks and silk. Spread the sweet corn with butter and season to taste with salt. Place on a grill 6–9 inches (15–23 cm) above medium hot coals and cook for 15–20 minutes, turning and basting regularly with the remaining butter.

Method 2

Remove the corn husks and silk and rinse well in salted iced water. Place each cob on a sheet of extra-thick aluminium foil and brush with ½ oz (15 g) of softened butter. Sprinkle 1 tbsp water over the corn, wrap securely and place in the barbecue coals for about 15 minutes, turning several times.

Method 3

Remove the outer corn husk, turn back the inner husks and remove the silk and rinse well in salted iced water. Brush the corn generously with Garlic Butter (see p. 127). Replace husks over cob and hold them in place with hoops of fine wire (position the wire near each end and in the centre). Roast on the barbecue grill over hot coals for about 20 minutes, turning every 3–5 minutes. To serve, cut the wire and remove the husks (good heat-resistant gloves will be needed for this job).

Method 4

Strip off the husks and silk. Remove the rind from a rasher of fat bacon, wrap the bacon around the corn and secure with cocktail sticks previously soaked in cold water. Grill over hot coals for about 20 minutes, turning frequently, or until the bacon is nice and crisp and the uncovered areas of the corn are golden brown.

A selection of foil-wrapped vegetables for barbecuing including (clockwise from top) runner beans, brussel sprouts, asparagus spears, broad beans, sliced carrots, broccoli, sliced courgettes, peas with mushroom slices.

Orange Butter Glazed Carrots

Serves 4–6

2 lb (0·9 kg) new carrots, scrubbed or scraped
2 oranges
3 oz (85 g) butter
3 tbsp brown sugar

Parboil the carrots in salted water until just tender but still crisp. Drain well. Grate the rind from the oranges and extract the juice. Combine the orange rind, orange juice, butter and brown sugar in a saucepan and heat gently until the sugar has dissolved. Bring the mixture to the boil and simmer gently for 5 minutes. Dip the carrots in the mixture and barbecue over medium coals for 5 minutes basting occasionally with the remaining sauce.

Stuffed Peppers

Serves 6

6 large green peppers
4 oz (115 g) Cheddar cheese
1½ lb (0·7 kg) cooked haricot beans
Hot and Tasty Barbecue Sauce (see p. 124)
oregano
pinch garlic salt
ground black pepper

Slice the tops from the peppers, remove the seeds and rinse well. Grate the cheese and put approximately 1 oz (30 g) to one side. Mix the remainder of the cheese with the beans, stir in half the sauce and lightly season with oregano, garlic salt and pepper. Fill the peppers with the bean mixture and top each with 1 tbsp sauce.

Wrap each pepper securely in a double thickness of extra-thick aluminium foil and grill over hot coals for 30–40 minutes, turning occasionally. Just before serving, open the foil packages and sprinkle the remaining cheese over the top of each pepper.

Spit-roasted leg of lamb (p. 84).

Vegetable Kebabs

Serves 6

6 small potatoes
6 small onions
12 medium mushrooms
2 green peppers
2 oz (55 g) butter, melted
½ tsp garlic salt
¼ tsp ground black pepper
6 small tomatoes

Peel the potatoes and onions and cook, separately, in boiling salted water until barely tender. Remove the stems from the mushrooms and wash the caps. Remove the seeds from the peppers and cut them into twelve pieces. Drain the onions and potatoes and thread on to six skewers alternating with the pieces of pepper and mushroom caps. Blend the melted butter, salt and pepper together, and brush the kebabs generously with the mixture.

Cook with the grill set about 4–5 inches (10–13 cm) above hot coals. After 5 minutes add a tomato to each skewer, turn kebabs over and brush with more of the mixture. Continue cooking for another 5 minutes.

Stuffed Aubergine

Serves 8

2 medium to large aubergines
2 large onions, finely chopped
3 tbsp parsley, chopped
¼ tsp garlic salt
¼ tsp oregano
6 oz (170 g) butter or margarine
⅛ tsp ground black pepper
salt
juice of 1 lemon

Halve the aubergines lengthwise and sprinkle a little salt and lemon juice over the exposed flesh. Let the aubergines stand for about 30 minutes and then pour off any liquid that has formed. Scoop out and dice the flesh and then combine it with the chopped onions, parsley, garlic salt and oregano. Simmer the mixture in the butter or margarine until the onions and aubergine pulp are tender. Season to taste with the black pepper, salt and remainder of the lemon juice. Stuff the aubergine skins with the mixture and put the halves together.

Securely seal the reassembled vegetables in extra-thick foil and grill over hot coals, turning occasionally, for about 40 minutes or until the aubergine feels soft. Cooking the aubergines directly among the hot coals will reduce the cooking time by approximately 10 minutes.

To serve, cut the aubergines into quarters.

Ratatouille

Serves 4–6

1 medium aubergine, sliced	2 cloves garlic, crushed
2 medium to large onions	1 tbsp fresh basil or 1 tsp dried
4 small courgettes	1 tsp dried rosemary
1 medium green pepper	1 bay leaf
1 medium red pepper	½ tsp ground black pepper
2 tomatoes	1 tsp salt
6 tbsp oil	2 tbsp parsley, chopped

First prepare the vegetables. Thinly slice the aubergine, onions and courgettes; de-seed and chop the red and green peppers; and peel and de-seed the tomatoes, cutting them into wedges.

Place a large skillet on the barbecue and heat the oil. Add the onions and crushed garlic and cook for about 5 minutes or until the onion becomes soft and translucent. Next add the aubergine, red and green peppers and the courgettes. Cook for another 5 minutes, shaking the skillet frequently. Add the tomatoes, basil, rosemary, bay leaf and seasoning. Sprinkle with parsley. Place the cover on the barbecue and cook for about 1 hour. Serve hot or cold as a main dish or with chicken, lamb, fish or beef.

Roasted Aubergine

Serves 4–6

1 medium aubergine
2 oz (55 g) melted butter or margarine
salt
ground black pepper

Prick the aubergine all over with a two-tined fork. Brush with the melted butter or margarine and sprinkle with salt. Place on greased grill over the drip pan centred on a lower charcoal grill. Place the cover on the barbecue and bake for 20–30 minutes or until tender. Turn once during cooking.

To serve, cut slices about ½ inch (1 cm) thick. Brush them with melted butter or margarine and sprinkle with more salt and ground black pepper.

Stuffed Tomatoes

Serves 4

2 large, firm tomatoes
3 tbsp fresh white breadcrumbs
2 tbsp parsley, finely chopped
⅛ tsp garlic powder
1 oz (30 g) grated cheese (Cheddar, mozzarella or to choice)
2 tbsp softened butter
pinch dried basil

Cut the tomatoes in half crosswise and scrape out the seeds using a teaspoon. Combine the remaining ingredients and lightly pack the mixture into the tomato cavities.

Position tomatoes, cut side up, on a grill over medium hot coals and cook for about 10 minutes or until the tomatoes are heated through and the cheese has melted.

Christine's Barbecued Baked Beans   *(Plate 6)*

Serves 4–6

4 oz (115 g) streaky bacon
1 oz (25 g) butter
1 tbsp oil
1 large onion, finely chopped
1 stick celery, finely chopped
15 oz (425 g) can of baked beans in tomato sauce

4 small frankfurter sausages
1 tbsp horseradish sauce
2 tbsp Worcestershire sauce
1 tsp French mustard
3 tbsp tomato ketchup
2 oz (55 g) dark soft brown sugar

Cut the bacon into pieces about 1 inch (2·5 cm) long and put into a heavy pan. Heat gently over the hot coals until the fat starts to run. Add the butter, oil, onion and celery and cook gently until the onion and celery have turned golden brown. Add the remaining ingredients to the pan and heat through while stirring frequently. If using a covered barbecue, leave the pan uncovered during the final heating period to give the surface of the beans a nice smoky flavour and crusty coating. If heating the beans on an open barbecue, keep the pan covered when the mixture is not being stirred.

Plate 6 shows a large quantity of Christine's Barbecued Baked Beans (20 cans!) being cooked in a stainless steel pan incorporated into the new modular barbecue (for further details see pp. 11–13).

Grilled Bananas République

Serves 6

6 medium ripe bananas
3 oz (85 g) butter, melted
2 tbsp lemon juice
¼ tsp ground ginger
¼ tsp ground cloves
pinch cinnamon or nutmeg

Place the whole unpeeled bananas on the food grill 4 inches (10 cm) from the coals. Cook for 4–5 minutes or until the skins turn black. Turn the bananas over and cook for a further 4–5 minutes.

Combine the butter, lemon juice, ginger and cloves. When the bananas are ready, carefully run the sharp point of a knife down both sides of each (try to avoid cutting into the flesh) and peel off the top half of the skin. Spoon the spiced butter over the top of each banana and sprinkle with cinnamon or nutmeg.

Serve piping hot with barbecued ham, pork or chicken.

Bananas Diana

Serves 6

6 large firm bananas
4 oz (115 g) butter or margarine, melted
3 tbsp orange juice
1 tbsp clear honey
1 tsp ground ginger
1 tsp lemon juice
2 oz (55 g) brown sugar
3 tbsp rum (optional)
whipped cream or vanilla ice-cream
2 tbsp flaked coconut

Peel bananas, cut in half lengthwise and arrange in a shallow baking tin.

Combine butter or margarine, orange juice, honey, ground ginger, lemon juice, brown sugar and rum; mix well. Spoon the sauce over the bananas.

Centre tin on cooking grill; place cover on barbecue and heat for about 12 minutes, or until just tender (do not overcook). Baste with the sauce two or three times during cooking.

Serve hot, topped with whipped cream or ice-cream and sprinkled with flaked coconut.

Brenda's Pineapple Flambé

Serves 4

1 fresh pineapple, or 8 slices tinned pineapple
6 tbsp clear honey
2 tbsp white rum
whipped cream or ice-cream

Remove the skin of the pineapple and cut out the hard fibrous centre. Slice into eight rings. Grill the rings over hot coals for about 2–3 minutes each side, basting frequently with the honey.

Place the cooked pineapple rings on a serving dish and sprinkle them with the rum. Set the rum alight and serve immediately with cream or ice-cream.

Ron and Pam's Stuffed Pears

Serves 6

6 comice pears (with stalks)

Stuffing
2 oz (55 g) unsalted butter
1 oz (30 g) castor sugar
1 oz (30 g) ground almonds

1 lemon
1 oz (30 g) glacé cherries, finely chopped
pinch of cinnamon
1 tsp kirsch
single cream

Cream together the butter and sugar. Add the ground almonds, grated rind from the lemon, finely chopped glacé cherries and a pinch of cinnamon. Add the kirsch and mix well. Squeeze the juice from the lemon into a saucer and put to one side. If necessary, trim the base of the pears so that they can stand upright. Peel the pears leaving stalks intact. Stand each pear in the saucer of lemon juice in turn and brush the surface liberally with the juice. Cut the top off each pear about 1 inch (2.5 cm) below base of the stalk and reserve. Scoop out the cores and stuff the cavities with the prepared mixture. Replace the tops. Stand each pear in the centre of a piece of lightly buttered foil approximately 9 inches (23 cm) square. Pour the remainder of the lemon juice over the pears. Dust with castor sugar and bring the edges of the foil up around each pear, twisting securely around to cover the pear but leaving the stalk free.

Stand the packages in a shallow baking tin or double-thickness sheet of foil with the edges turned up. Cook for approximately 40 minutes, by either the direct or indirect method. The pears are ready if they feel soft inside when gently pressed with a gloved hand or tongs.

Serve in foil on individual sweet dishes allowing guests to open package and add cream as desired.

SEASONINGS, MARINADES, SAUCES AND FLAVOURED BUTTERS

Seasonings

Seasonings of any kind are meant to enhance the flavour of food, not to overpower it, and meat and fish that have been barbecued in their natural juices should in fact need very little, if any, additional flavouring. The exceptions to this rule are, of course, specific dishes based on curry and chilli.

Seasoning should be varied to suit individual taste, but the judicious use of carefully selected spices, herbs and commercial seasonings will help to improve marginally (for that is all that should be aimed for) the aroma, colour and flavour of the food. A sure sign of the spreading popularity of barbecuing is the availability of seasonings especially developed for food being prepared for, or being cooked on, the barbecue.

Seasonings that are spice based, i.e. made from dried and ground aromatic seeds, roots, bark and so on, require a light and careful hand while herbs from the more temperate regions of the world are subtle enough to be used in slightly larger amounts. Herbs in fact are relatively easy to grow and apart from one or two – rosemary, for example, which is more akin to a bush than a plant – they take up very little room. The keen barbecue chef should therefore endeavour to cultivate a small, selective herb garden within plucking distance of the barbecue. If you haven't a garden you can cultivate herbs equally well in a tub or window box. Herbs have many uses for both the indoor and outdoor chef. They can be rubbed on to meat, inserted into meat (for example, barbecued lamb is delicious cooked with rosemary and slivers of garlic pushed into slits cut in the flesh), used as a marinade or sauce ingredient or – for the outdoor chef only – added to the fire to produce a wonderful aromatic smoke.

If I had to make a personal choice of just one herb to grow and use for barbecuing it would have to be rosemary. Even the branches of this versatile plant can be used: stripped of all but the end leaves, they make rather exotic skewers for kebabs. My other favourites are thyme and of course garlic, although it is simpler to buy garlic when required from the greengrocer. Other herbs that are particularly useful to the cook are marjoram, sage, tarragon, bay leaves (a bay tree looks very handsome when grown in a tub) and chives. Fresh herbs should be used whenever possible, but there is a wide and excellent choice of dried herbs easily available.

Marinades

Like the seasonings mentioned above, basting sauces and marinades have an important role to play in the preparation of certain meats. Apart from imparting moistness to very lean meat, the prime function of a marinade is to tenderize and enhance the flavour of those cuts which require something extra to make them more palatable. Properly marinated before cooking, an economic cut of beef will take on some of the attributes of the more expensive cuts. One should, however, whenever possible buy meat of the highest quality to ensure the best results.

The acid in a marinade (lemon, vinegar, wine, pineapple juice) acts as a tenderizing agent while the fat (oil, melted butter or margarine) helps to prevent lean meats from drying out when cooked over hot coals. One should therefore use an oily marinade on lean foods and the non-oily marinades (wine or vinegar based) on foods with a high fat content.

Some foods require very little marinating while others should be kept in the marinade for up to 24 hours or so in a refrigerator. The recipes give guidance about times. If the quantity of marinade you have made up is insufficient to cover the meat fully, it will be necessary to turn it several times to allow the flavour to penetrate more evenly. An easy way to achieve this is to place the marinade and meat in a strong plastic bag which should be tightly sealed. It is then a simple matter to coat the meat with the marinade and not the kitchen floor! As a safeguard against leaks, place the bag in a baking tin.

Having marinated the food, it should be removed from the marinade, drained of excess liquid and allowed to come to room temperature before barbecuing. The left-over marinade can be used as a baste while the meat is cooking, or stored in the refrigerator in an airtight container for future use.

Sauces

The word 'sauce' is often used in the same context as the word 'marinade' or 'baste'. A cooking sauce however, should contain oil, melted butter or margarine to keep the meat moist and incorporate various seasonings to impart flavour. Care should be taken when brushing or spooning sauces over meat, and poultry in particular, that it is not applied too soon or too thickly as the surface of the meat may burn and become over-flavoured as a result.

Sauces that have to be applied warm can be kept on the grill, adjacent to the food, in fire-proof containers.

Flavoured Butters

Garlic butter is perhaps the seasoned butter most often used in barbecuing and everyday cooking. It is certainly my favourite, especially when spread generously on hot French bread.

Because flavoured butters can be made up a day or so before a party (and kept in the refrigerator in a covered dish) they are a boon for the busy cook; at the same time they allow guests to add a distinctive flavour of their own choice to plain grilled fish, steaks, burgers, chicken pieces, lamb chops or vegetables and fruit. An assortment of two or three butters will provide sufficient choice. Some varieties of flavoured butters will also make a tasty and fairly economic sandwich spread. Margarine can be used instead of butter in most of these recipes.

Teriyaki Marinade

1½ tbsp honey or 2 tbsp brown sugar
1½ tbsp oil
4 tbsp soy sauce
¾ tbsp dry red wine or red wine vinegar
1 tsp freshly grated ginger or ⅕ tsp ginger powder
1 clove garlic, crushed

Combine all the ingredients and pour over the food. Refrigerate, turning occasionally.

Use for poultry, beef, spare-ribs and fish, and also as a basting sauce. Chicken and spare-ribs should be marinated for 4–8 hours; beef for 8 hours; fish for 2–4 hours.

Soy-lemon Marinade

6 tbsp lemon juice
6 tbsp soy sauce
4 tbsp oil
½ tsp ground black pepper
1 clove garlic, crushed
1 bay leaf

Combine all the ingredients and allow to stand for 1–2 hours before use.

This is excellent for joints of beef which can be marinated in a heavy-duty plastic bag in a refrigerator for up to three days. The meat should be turned frequently during this period. Drain well before roasting.

Mint Marinade

1½ tbsp mint leaves (minced)
½ pt (280 ml) dry white wine
4 tbsp oil
1 clove garlic, crushed
¼ tsp ground black pepper
¼ tsp crushed basil
¾ tbsp minced parsley (fresh or dried)
½ tsp salt
1 tsp sugar

Combine all the ingredients well, pour over the food and leave for 2–3 hours. These quantities will make about ½pt (280ml) of marinade.

Use with lamb or chicken.

Honey with Mint Marinade

¼ pt (140 ml) dry white wine
4 tbsp clear honey
2 tsp fresh mint, chopped
1 tbsp wine vinegar
1 clove garlic, crushed
1 tsp salt

Combine all the ingredients well and allow to stand for about an hour before use.

Use with lamb or chicken.

Red Wine Marinade

½ pt (280 ml) dry red wine
1 tsp dried whole basil or oregano
2 cloves garlic, crushed
1 tsp salt
2 tbsp wine vinegar
1½ tbsp melted butter or oil

Combine all the ingredients and heat in a saucepan until the marinade starts to simmer. Remove from the heat immediately, cover the pan and allow to stand for about an hour. Pour over the meat (this is best with pork or beef) and marinate for 2–5 hours, according to taste.

Seafare Marinade

¼ pt (140 ml) dry white wine
3 tbsp oil
1 tsp paprika
½ tsp salt
⅛ tsp ground black pepper
1 tsp sugar
¾ tbsp minced parsley

Combine all the ingredients and pour over seafood. There should be sufficient marinade to cover approximately 2 lb (0·9 kg).

Hot and Tasty Barbecue Sauce

3 tbsp Worcestershire sauce
1 tsp chilli powder
1 tsp dry mustard
1 tsp salt
1 tsp ground black pepper
4 tbsp honey

½ pt (280 ml) chilli sauce
300 ml tomato ketchup
2 drops tabasco
3 tbsp wine vinegar
3 tbsp tarragon vinegar

Mix all the ingredients together with 6 tbsp water. Add a little more water if it is too thick.

Use with chicken, hamburgers and steak. This sauce is particularly good for basting ribs during the last few minutes of cooking.

Sweet and Sour Sauce

¼ pt (140 ml) dry white wine
1½ tbsp white wine vinegar
1½ tbsp oil
½ pt (280 ml) crushed pineapple
   (undrained)
1 tbsp soy sauce

1 tsp lemon juice
¼ tsp garlic salt
½ tsp dry mustard
1½ tbsp brown sugar
¾ tbsp chopped onion (optional)

Combine all the ingredients, mixing well, and simmer in a saucepan for about 10–15 minutes.

Use to baste poultry, pork, lamb, ribs and fish steaks.

Horseradish and Cream Sauce

Serves 4–6

¼ pt (140 ml) double cream
1 tbsp lemon juice
1 tsp horseradish sauce
2 tsp Worcestershire sauce
2 spring onions, finely chopped

Mix together the double cream and lemon juice. Blend in remaining ingredients. Allow to stand for at least 4 hours.

Serve with barbecued steaks and hamburgers or use as a topping for jacket potatoes.

Indonesian Sauce

Serves 4–6

1 tbsp oil
4 tbsp (level) peanut butter
¼ pt (140 ml) tomato ketchup
3 tbsp Worcestershire sauce
garlic powder to taste
¼ tsp salt

Heat the oil gently in a pan and add the peanut butter. Continue heating gently, stirring occasionally until the peanut butter begins to thicken and darkens slightly. Remove from the heat immediately and stir in the tomato ketchup and Worcestershire sauce. Season to taste with garlic powder and salt. Allow to stand for 2 hours before use. Reheat gently, and add a little water if the sauce is too thick.

Serve with barbecued chicken and steaks; it can also be used to baste chicken.

Spicy Orange Sauce

Serves 4–6

4 tbsp soy sauce
6 tbsp orange juice
6 tbsp soft brown sugar
8 tbsp dry white wine
½ tsp dry mustard
½ tsp paprika

2 drops tabasco
1 shallot, finely chopped
pinch ground cinnamon
2 tsp cornflour
salt and pepper

Mix together the first nine ingredients with 3 tbsp water and bring slowly to the boil, stirring continuously. Simmer for 5–6 minutes, then thicken with the cornflour. Season with salt and pepper to taste.

Orange and Honey Butter

Cream ¼ lb (115 g) softened butter with 1 tbsp orange juice, 1 tbsp grated orange peel, 1 tbsp honey, 2 tsp finely chopped parsley.

Serve with lamb, duck or chicken.

Lemon Butter

Cream ¼ lb (115 g) softened butter or margarine with 2 tbsp lemon juice and 1 tsp finely grated lemon peel.

Spread over seafood, poultry or vegetables. Melt before using as a basting sauce.

Tarragon and Parsley Butter

Cream ¼ lb (115 g) softened butter until light and fluffy. Blend in ½ tsp grated lemon peel, 2 tsp lemon juice, 1 tbsp finely chopped parsley, ¼ tsp salt and ¼ tsp dried, crushed tarragon.

Excellent for seasoning grilled steaks.

Garlic Butter

Cream ¼ lb (115 g) butter or margarine with 1 tsp finely minced garlic and 1½ tbsp minced parsley.

Spread on seafood, grilled lamb chops, beef steaks, hot French bread or boiled new potatoes.

Danish Blue Butter

Combine ¼ lb (115 g) butter or margarine with ¼ lb (115 g) of crumbled Danish blue cheese, ¼ tsp paprika, and 2 tbsp double cream. Beat until light and fluffy.

Excellent when melted on steaks or hamburgers. It can also be used as a filling for baked potatoes, and makes an appetizing sandwich spread.

Herb Butter

Cream ¼ lb (115 g) softened butter or magarine with ½ tsp tarragon or rosemary, 1 tbsp finely chopped chives, ¾ tbsp minced parsley, ⅛–¼ tsp of salt and a pinch of pepper.

Use with cooked vegetables, poultry, seafood and poached eggs. Try it as a sandwich spread.

Maître d'Hôtel Butter

Combine ¼ lb (115 g) butter, 2 tsp minced parsley, ¼ tsp salt, 2 tsp lemon juice, ¼ tsp thyme and a pinch of ground black pepper. Beat until light and fluffy.

Excellent for seasoning cooked vegetables and sautéd fish, or as a baste for grilled or roasted chicken.

Cooking Time-charts

1. Grilling

Food type	Cut	Size or weight	Recommended fire-heat	Approximate cooking time (each side) in minutes		
				rare	medium	well done
Beef	steak	1 inch (2·5 cm)	hot	5–6	7–8	10–12
	steak*	1½ inches (4 cm)	hot	6–7	9–10	12–15
	flank steak	whole	hot	4–5†		
	hamburger	1 inch (2·5 cm)	medium	3–4	5–6	7–10
	skewer		hot	4–5	6–8	10–12
Lamb	chops	1 inch (2·5 cm)	medium	5–6	7–8	10
	skewer		medium	5–6	7–8	10
Pork	chops	¾–1 inch (2–2·5 cm)	medium			18–20
	spare-ribs	whole	low/medium			1–1¼ hrs
	skewer		medium			15–20
Poultry	chicken	split	medium			35–45
	duck	split	medium	5–6	10–11	25
Veal	steaks or chops	1 inch (2·5 cm)	medium			9–12
	skewer		medium			10–15
Fish	steak	½ inch (1 cm)	medium			3–4
	steak	1 inch (2·5 cm)	medium			5–7
	fillets	¾ inch (2 cm)	medium			5–7
Lobster	split	1–1½ lb (450 g–0·7 kg)	medium/hot			14–15
Ham	slice	1 inch (2·5 cm)	medium			15–20

*If steaks are 2 inches (5 cm) or more thick you can use a meat thermometer. Steak is rare at 130°F (55°C) well done at 170°F (75°C).
†Maximum cooking time for meat to be tender.

2. Spit-roasting

Food type	Cut	Size or weight	Recommended fire-heat	Approximate cooking time in hours*		
				rare	medium	well done
				140°F (60°C)	160°F (70°C)	190°F (90°C)
Beef	rump (rolled)	3–5 lb (1·4–2·3 kg)	medium	1½–2	2¼–3	3–4
	sirloin	5–6 lb (2·3–2·7 kg)	medium/hot	1¼–1¾	2¼–3	3–4
	rolled rib	4–6 lb (1·8–2·7 kg)	medium/hot	2–2½	2¼–3	3¼–4½
				140°F (60°C)	160°F (70°C)	185°F (85°C)
Lamb	leg	3½–8 lb (1·6–3·6 kg)	medium	1–1¼	1½–2	2–3¼
	rolled shoulder	3–6 lb (1·4–2·7 kg)	medium	1–1¼	1½–2	2–3¼
						190°F (90°C)
Pork	shoulder	3–6 lb (1·4–2·7 kg)	medium			2–3
	loin	3–5 lb (1·4–2·3 kg)	medium			2–3
	spare-ribs	2–4 lb (0·9–1·8 kg)	medium/hot			1–1¾
	fresh ham	5–8 lb (2·3–3·6 kg)	medium			3½–4½
						190°F (90°C)
Poultry	chicken	2½–5 lb (1·1–2·3 kg)	medium			1–1½
	turkey	10–18 lb (4·5–8·2 kg)	medium			2–4
	duckling	4–6 lb (1·8–2·7 kg)	medium			1–2
						190°F (90°C)
Veal	leg	5–8 lb (2·3–3·6 kg)	medium			2–3
	rolled shoulder	3–5 lb (1·4–2·3 kg)	medium			1½–2½
	loin	5–6 lb (2·3–2·7 kg)	medium			1½–2½
						120–130°F (50–55°C)
Fish	large, whole	5–10 lb (2·3–4·5 kg)	low/medium			1–1¾
	small, whole	1½–4 lb (0·7–1·8 kg)	low/medium			½–1

*For accuracy use a meat thermometer and cook to the internal temperature given in the chart.

3. Roasting (for covered barbecues)

Food type	Cut	Readiness	Internal temperature	Approximate minutes per pound (450 g)
Beef	rib roast	rare	140°F (60°C)	18–20
		medium	160°F (70°C)	20–25
		well done	170°F (75°C)	25–30
	sirloin		140–170°F (60–75°C)	25–30
	rump/rolled		150–170°F (65–75°C)	25–30
Lamb	leg	rare	140°F (60°C)	18–22
		medium	160°F (70°C)	22–28
		well done	170°F (75°C)	28–33
	crown roast	rare	140°F (60°C)	28–33
		medium	160°F (70°C)	33–38
		well done	170°F (75°C)	38–43
	shoulder	medium	160°F (70°C)	22–28
		well done	170°F (75°C)	28–33
Pork	loin	well done	185°F (85°C)	25–30
	fresh ham	well done	185°F (85°C)	20–25
	crown	well done	185°F (85°C)	25–30
Veal	loin	well done	185°F (85°C)	20–25
	leg	well done	185°F (85°C)	20–25
	shoulder	well done	185°F (85°C)	20–25
Poultry	chicken	well done	185°F (85°C)	18–20
	turkey	well done	185°F (85°C)	12–20*
	duckling	well done	185°F (85°C)	15–20

*Cooking times will vary greatly according to weight of bird.

4. Foil-wrapped vegetables

Vegetable	Minutes (approx.)	
	Fresh	Frozen
artichoke hearts		20–25
asparagus (whole or 2 inch/5 cm pieces)	10–20	10–20
aubergine (peeled and cut in 1 inch/2·5 cm cubes)	30–40	
beans: French, runner (whole or 1½ inch/45 cm pieces)	20–35	20–30
broccoli (flowerets and stem) (whole or 2 inch/5 cm pieces)	15–20	20–22
Brussels sprouts	20–25	25–30
carrots (sliced crosswise or quartered lengthwise)	30–45	
cauliflower (flowerets)	15–20	20–22
courgettes (sliced or quartered lengthwise)	25–30	
mushrooms (whole or sliced)	8–12	
peas (shelled)	15–20	15–20
peas and carrots		15–20
sweet corn	20–25	25–30

Index of Recipes

	⊘	↦	⌓
herring, grilled with fennel, 108	●		
kebabs, *see* shish-kebabs			
kidneys, lamb			
and sausage kebabs, 85	●		
brochette with sauce Bercy, 84	●		
lamb, 81			
Andalusian chops, 82	●		
barbecue crown roast, 81			●
cinnamon cutlets, 83	●		
cumingon kebabs, 83	●		
kidney and sausage kebabs, 85	●		
kidney brochette with sauce Bercy, 84	●		
pineapple burgers, 85	●		
spicy kebabs, 86	●		
spit-roasted glazed shoulder, 82		●	
spit-roasted leg, 84		●	
spit-roasted stuffed leg, 81		●	
lemon butter, 127			
mackerel, cheesy crusted, 110	●		
maître d'hôtel butter, 128			
marinades, 120			
honey with mint, 123			
mint, 122			
red wine, 123			
seafare, 124			
soy-lemon, 122			
teriyaki, 121			
mullet, red, grilled with fennel, 106	●		
mussels, grilled, 105	●		
orange and honey butter, 127			
pears, Ron and Pam's stuffed, 118	●		
peppers, stuffed, 113	●		
pheasant, barbecued, 104			●
pig, barbecued sucking, 93–4		●	
pineapple, Brenda's flambé, 118	●		
pork, 86			
barbecued sucking pig, 93–4			
glazed roast loin, 89			
hot cheesy kebabs, 86	●		
Jeannie's pork and apricot kebabs, 92	●		